MW01292399

The Gift:
Finding the Extraordinary
in Everyday Living

By
Kathy Morley

The Gift: Finding the Extraordinary in Everyday Living.

Copyright © 2019 Kathy Morley

All rights reserved. No part of this book may be used or reproduced in any manner whatsoever without written permission from the author, except by a reviewer who may quote brief passages in a review.
Techniques discussed in this book are intended as an informational guide. They may supplement, not be a substitute for, professional medical care or treatment.

ISBN: 978-1-09886-834-5

Cassie Publishing
To contact the author, email CassiePublishing@gmail.com

Cover design by Beau Lethbridge

Contents

Dedication...vii

Acknowledgements...ix

Introduction...xi

PART I: Emergence of the Healer

Chapter 1: Su Casa...3

Chapter 2: Perry...16

Chapter 3: Grandma Rose and Mom...23

Chapter 4: Su Casa Revisited...27

Chapter 5: Table Tipping...30

Chapter 6: Meditation...35

Chapter 7: The Shekinah Fire...38

PART II: Receiving and Transmitting Energy

Chapter 8: UFO's...45

Chapter 9: Dr. Gilda...48

Chapter 10: Reiki...55

Chapter 11: College Health Fair...58

Chapter 12 Danielle...61

Chapter 13: Brenda...64

Chapter 14: Reconnecting with White Eagle...65

Chapter 15: Millie...69

PART III: ARE Conferences

Chapter 16: Finding my Mission in Life...75

Chapter 17: We Don't Die...83

PART IV: Bridging Two Worlds Through Hypnosis

Chapter 18: Candy...97

Chapter 19: Dungeon of Despair...100

Chapter 20: John...103

Chapter 21: Ellie...111

Chapter 22: George...116

Chapter 23: Barbara...119

Chapter 24: Antonitus...123

PART V: Comfort and Confirmation

Chapter 25: Janie...169

Chapter 26: Annette...171

Chapter 27: Victor and Coleen...172

Chapter 28: Lynn...173

Chapter 29: Deidra...176

Chapter 30: Sue...177

PART VI: Channeling...185

PART VII: Epilogue...193

Glossary...195

Suggested Reading...196

Dedication

This book is dedicated to my greatest teacher, my daughter Kristine, who through her mental illness taught me unconditional love and compassion as well as deep heartache.

Acknowledgements

Special thanks to Judi Davis, Ed.D. and Mark Kassop, Ph.D. for reading, offering feedback and encouraging me to finish my manuscript years ago. Grateful acknowledgement goes to Gerry Bowman, an incredible psychic and medium for his readings and guidance over the years. I treasure the friendship I shared with him and John, the spirit he channeled. Gerry has since passed on. Appreciation goes out to the Cornwall Writers Group for their critiquing and wisdom.

Deep appreciation goes to Carmela O'Flaherty for her editing, and invaluable input. I especially thank my husband, Steve, for his endless love and support. Lastly, I am honored to be facilitator of the personal experiences of the people chronicled in this book.

Introduction

The Gift: Finding the Extraordinary in Everyday Living is about my healing journey which spans from the early nineties to the present. What began as routine journaling, became a survival mechanism in my bleakest hours and a chronicling of my deepest joy. It's about rising up from the ashes to living one step beyond the parameters of the physical world, and reawakening childlike curiosity and openness, leading to the realization that anything is possible.

My incredible experiences gave me hope when there was little. They lifted me out of despair precipitated by divorce and my daughter's mental illness. Although my daughter's lifelong struggle with such a debilitating and insidious disease had a major impact on my life, that is not what this book is about; the resulting spiritual growth is. It's about becoming aware of the many innate intuitive abilities available to each and every one of us but like a muscle, needs to be exercised.

Along with my sharpened intuitive abilities, I began to believe in mind/body healing techniques because of a medical crisis that led me to seek training in alternative methods of healing. Endometriosis had ravaged my pelvic area. A year after the initial surgery, a second was recommended. I refused and sought a natural solution. I learned biofeedback and used visualizations resulting in complete remission of the disease. That incredible experience helped me reclaim my power and taught me that I could be a participant in the health of my body. As a result, I want others to be able to do the same. By sharing the stories in this book, I hope readers will leave the door open to experience the extraordinary in their lives. The accounts in this book are real, although some of the names and places have been changed.

As you walk with me on my journey, you will be introduced to energies that enriched my life such as meditation, Reiki, hypnosis, past life regression, and the Shekinah Fire. Through the maze of life, I realize that our lives are our voyage back to wholeness. And as you read on, I ask that you be receptive to new possibilities. With openness, comes the opportunity to experience the unexpected and enhance your life.

Part I: Emergence of the Healer

Chapter One

Su Casa

I find it amazing that when I am able to let go of controlling my life and just allow it to unfold, it flows like a perfect symphony. The summer of 1991 was one of those times where my mind, body and soul were in perfect harmony. I felt it in every fiber of my being. There was so much upheaval and stress in my life that I just surrendered. That's when my life took a 180-degree turn, opening up and blossoming like a tulip in the morning sun.

Although my journey in this incarnation began at my birth, over sixty years ago, my Spirit was truly awakened in the nineties. This chapter of my life began on a sunny afternoon; Mary and I were sitting basking in the sun, on the porch of her beautiful old Victorian house. Over a glass of iced tea, I asked what she had planned for the weekend.

"I'm going up to Su Casa for a New Age weekend." She offered me a blueberry scone.

I broke off a piece and took a bite. "What's that about?"

"You know, psychics, crystals, tarot, massage therapy." Her eyes widened. "Why don't you come with me? Experience it for yourself."

I frowned.

"Are you afraid?"

Her question startled me. "Of course not!" I snapped. I just don't know if I would like it. That's all." I didn't want to admit that I was.

"How do you know unless you try it? Come on, it will be loads of fun. Don't be such a stick in the mud. Kathy, step out of the box!"

I burst out laughing. "Okay, okay. I have no plans for the weekend anyway." If nothing else, I thought to myself, the weekend would be entertaining.

Since Mary was going to the Omega Institute after our weekend trip, we took separate cars. Approaching the hotel, I couldn't contain my surprise. The resort looked more like an old run-down adolescent summer camp. The parking area was a rocky, uneven dirt road. As I opened my car door, and stood up, weeds sprang up around my knees. I looked around. There were small old bungalows scattered around, with one larger building. *Resort? What the hell is this, some kind of joke? Never mind paying for this hole in the wall! I wouldn't stay here if I were paid.* My first instinct was to get in my car and head for home. Instead, I waited for Mary to show up so that I could wring her little neck! Walking around mumbling to myself, I came across a man sitting on a bench. He was in his early fifties, with salt and pepper hair. He looked up from his newspaper as I walked by.

"Hi. I'm Gerry." He smiled, stood up and gave me a warm handshake.

I managed a faint smile. "Kathy."

"First time here?"

"Yeah," I replied meekly.

He chuckled. "I could tell by the expression on your face. Why, the first time I came up here, I thought the same thing you are thinking right now. But you know what? I love it here. The people are wonderful, warm and very open. Whenever I'm feeling super-stressed and need to get away, I come up here to unwind - usually a few times a year."

"Quite honestly, I was contemplating leaving before my friend gets here."

"Do yourself a favor." He gently touched my arm. "Forget how this place looks. It's got great energy. It's magical. You'll see. Relax. Have fun. Kathy, enjoy the people, enjoy the workshops." He had a confident look on his face. "Trust me, by the end of the weekend, you'll be planning your next trip back." He pointed to a door in need of a paint job. "Go ahead. Go inside and register."

"Your jubilation makes me take pause about leaving."

"You won't be sorry," he insisted. "Breathe in great country air, take scenic walks, and enjoy delicious food. All workshops are included too. Where else can you spend three days for a little over a hundred bucks?"

"Nowhere," I answered with a forced smile and walked up the steps. "Thank God," I whispered under my breath.

Walking into the main building, I looked around for some signs of life. The first thing I noticed was a desk piled with clean white towels and a stack of travel-size soaps. A large room was off to my right. It was big, and sunlight streamed through the windows to the center of the room. There was a large stone fireplace, wood paneled walls, and parquet floors that had weathered many a year. My observation was interrupted when a diminutive woman in her sixties came out from a back room.

"Can I help you?" she queried with a smile that lit up her face.

"Yes. I'm Kathy. I'd like to check in and get my key."

"Well, you are in the right place. "I'm Maura, the owner. I'll give you your room number, but we don't have keys."

I thought I heard wrong. "No keys?"

"No."

"How do you lock your room?" I asked, controlling my annoyance.

"You don't. There's no need to lock rooms. Nothing has ever been stolen." She shrugged her shoulders. "But, if it will make you feel better, valuables can be locked in the office where there's a small safe." Without waiting for a response, she picked up two large towels, a small one, soap, and handed them to me. "You can get fresh ones every day. You're in room number thirteen in the first building to the right. Enjoy your stay."

I wanted to high tail it out of there. Instead, I remembered what Gerry had said and resisted the urge. I walked out of the main building supplies in hand and headed for my room. At that moment I saw Mary pulling into a parking spot, waving her hands at me.

"Hey, Kath!" she yelled excitedly through her car window. "I see you found the place."

"Yes. Lovely resort? A bit of an exaggeration, don't you think? Instead you should have told me, it was one step away from an abandoned site!"

My retort did not dampen her exuberance. Mary got out of her car and gave me a hug. "I'm sorry I didn't warn you, but I didn't want you to focus on that; it's a great place. I swear you'll have a good time. I'm going in to register. Catch you later."

Speechless, I watched Mary bolt up the stairs and into the building. Still apprehensive, I continued to my room.

That evening, we had a sumptuous dinner consisting of a hearty legume soup, fresh cooked veggies and whole grain bread. Surprisingly, people who were presenting a lecture or a workshop cooked the meals and cleaned up. They didn't pay for their stay nor did they get paid for their work. It was a great arrangement that kept the cost of the weekend down.

After dinner, I met Marilyn, who was getting ready to conduct a guided meditation. She was about 5'6", slender with long salt and pepper hair, a warm, captivating smile and soulful eyes. Marilyn explained she was a psychic and a trance channeler. Her Spirit Guide, Gene, spoke through her when she entered the trance state. I was skeptical but drawn to her. I couldn't quite put my finger on it, but Marilyn had an unexplainable charisma and charm.

Before the meditation, Marilyn led us through stretching exercises to help us relax. We were told to alternately tense and relax each part of our body. She continued with a guided visualization. "Gently close your eyes and take a deep breath inhaling way down into the bottom of your belly. Now exhale any stress and negativity." Her out breath made an audible whooshing sound. "Feel the air as it makes its way up your nose, down your throat, into your lungs, feeling your diaphragm expanding. Then, as you exhale, feel the diaphragm contracting and the air rising in your lungs, into your throat and out your nose. Continue this for a few more breaths."

Two minutes passed. "Now imagine a magnificent white light coming down from the heavens and going in through the top of your head, down your spine, all the way through your body, relaxing as it goes down through to your feet. Now imagine roots coming out the bottom of your feet going all the way down into the ground rooting you to mother earth. Now as I count back from ten to one, allow yourself to reach a deeper state of relaxation. Ten ... feeling more relaxed ... Nine ... your body is getting heavier as you relax deeper ... Eight ... going in deeper and deeper ... Two ... One. Take a few minutes and allow yourself to be in the present moment and go wherever your mind takes you."

Being a meditator for many years, getting into a relaxed state was easy. A few minutes later, I heard Marilyn's voice asking each one of us to say aloud where we were and what was going on. I was cognizant of what everyone was saying, while I stayed in my own space. One woman said she was on top of her house looking around. Another woman was in a tunnel and saw light at the end. She said she felt wonderful. A man saw colors, while another could not still himself enough to experience anything. Much to my amazement, I was face-to-face with some kind of beings. They were dark, standing very close to one another, looking at me. I felt like I was in a fishbowl. They seemed to be gently swaying.

Marilyn interrupted by asking, "Kathy, where are you?"

I was transfixed by the scene before me. I didn't want to talk, I just wanted to observe. Besides I wanted to keep my focus on them to see what they were going to do.

Marilyn asked again, "Kathy, where are you?"

I struggled to find my voice. "There are beings in front of me." *I am afraid to verbalize my mounting fear.*

Marilyn asked the revealing question. "Are they of this earth?"

Oh God, she knew. I'm afraid to answer.

She asked again.

I stuttered. "I don't think so."

"What are they doing, Kathy?" Marilyn gently prodded.

"They're just standing there, looking at me."

"Smile and be friendly."

I'm frozen with fear. I don't want to do or say anything to upset them. "I'm afraid."

"Don't be, just do it." Her voice was assertive yet comforting.

In my mind, I smiled and extended my hand. The small one in front lifted his little gray-blue hand and touched my fingers. The instant our fingers met was like being plugged into a television screen. I saw what seemed like a faraway galaxy. The place they came from. It was beautiful, clean and orderly. A kaleidoscope of colors. The buildings appeared suspended in the air. My vantage point was high off the ground as though I was effortlessly floating. I looked out at the expanse of the city. The magnificence of the panoramic view kept me spellbound. The fear had dissipated. It wasn't until later that I realized this was all transpiring telepathically.

Marilyn's voice interrupted my reverie. "All right folks, let's bring our consciousness back into the room."

Reluctantly, I opened my eyes. I pondered what had just happened. Had a curtain been lifted, allowing me to peek beyond the world that was familiar to me? I didn't know but was thirsting for more.

Bright and early on Saturday morning, I attended a yoga class under a large statuesque oak tree in front of the main building. The instructor, a woman in her sixties, had shoulder length dark brown hair pulled back in a ponytail. Her legs, from years of yogic postures, looked svelte under skintight leggings.

"Good morning everyone. My name is Dottie. We will start with a few warm up exercises but first let me say there are many different forms of yoga. I was trained in Hatha Yoga. 'Ha' translated means sun, while 'tha' means moon. 'Ha' is the masculine energy representing active, hot, sun while 'tha' represents the receptive, cool, moon energy in all of us. The objective is to balance the two energies."

After some stretches and breathing exercises, we were led through a string of poses, finishing with the corpse pose, where you lie on your back and relax your mind as well as every muscle. I felt relaxed and rejuvenated at the same time.

That morning, I also attended a class on crystals. I learned which crystals were good for healing, anxiety, transmuting negative energy and protection. It was informative and well-presented, but I wished Marilyn was presenting all the sessions. My unwavering interest and intrigue in her presentations surprised me.

In the evening, Marilyn led us through another guided meditation. I was anticipating another meeting with the beings I had encountered the day before. Much to my dismay, they didn't appear, but the meditation morphed into an exhilarating out-of-body experience. I became weightless, floating up and out of the building. Effortlessly, I rose higher and higher, picking up speed as I traveled over treetops. Then through puffs of clouds. I took a moment to glance at the land and sea below before I resumed my vertical climb into outer space.

Looking down, the earth was a tiny dot as I passed a myriad of space junk such as old pieces of satellites that orbit the earth. A black domed area came into view and like a curious kitten, I inched closer. Peering in, I lost my concentration and balance and fell in, descending rapidly. It was a large vacuum. *No air! How am I going to breathe?* I worked myself into a frenzy until I realized I didn't need air since I wasn't in my physical body. I started to calm down when I felt a pulling sensation, drawing me in deeper towards the darkness.

In sheer terror, I pushed against the energy and catapulted myself out. A whirlwind of colors, purple, white, silver, and black spun before me. Then came the visions. Flashes of a temple with a female sphinx. Earthquakes. Nuclear blasts out of the ground. Tsunamis ruining cities. Mushroom clouds spewing out of the ocean. Devastation at every turn. *Am I getting a glimpse of the future?*

When Marilyn brought us back, I revealed my visions.

"You're experiencing second sight," she offered.

"I can't shake the feeling of an overwhelming sense of grief and sadness. I'm beginning to think clairvoyance is a burden."

"That's because you are allowing yourself to feel the pain and suffering, Kathy. Just observe. Save the emotion for personal stuff. You'll be okay."

"I'll try." *There's so much to absorb. I mean, I've had one reality my whole life, and in just one weekend, it changed. For the very first time, I feel a different kind of excitement. One of anticipation and wonder.*

Time went fast. Before I knew it, Sunday lunch was over and everyone was ready to pack up and go home. In just two and a half days, we got to know one another very well. Marilyn and I exchanged telephone numbers and promised to keep in touch.

Gerry, the first guy I ran into, came over and gave me a hug. "What do you think of Su Casa now?" he cooed.

I took a deep breath and let out a sigh. "If it weren't for you, I wouldn't have stayed. This weekend was nothing short of magical, just like you said!"

That extraordinary weekend at Su Casa led me to reevaluate occurrences in my life that had no explanation and were labeled "coincidences." Growing up, my psychic experiences were squelched by responses like, "It's just your imagination," or "It was just a bad dream."

In the fifties, when I was seven, my parents bought an old home. One night in a dream, a man with a warm and gentle smile appeared to me. He told me he used to live in the house. He spoke of a fire in the house, although he assured me I was safe.

The next morning, upon awakening, I remembered my encounter. Frightened that a fire was going to take place, I told my parents about the dream. My fourteen-year-old brother Danny laughed and teased me while my parents dismissed it as a nightmare.

Validation came years later when I was a teenager. My older brother Frank, who lived in the second-floor apartment above my parents, decided to renovate the kitchen. He broke down walls and, lo and behold, there were burned cinder blocks, evidence there had been a fire.

For the rest of my adolescent years, psychic experiences were few, and even when I used my intuition, I was unaware of it. When I was twenty, every morning I dropped my then husband off at the train station to go to work.

One night, I had a vivid dream that after dropping him off, a car came flying out of a garage and hit me on the driver's side, smashing into my door. The driver, a chunky woman about fifty years old, with black wavy hair and black rimmed glasses, came out of her car and asked me if I was hurt. I was screaming as my husband woke me. I relayed the dream to him and expressed fear that it was going to happen.

"It's just a bad dream. Go back to sleep."

"But it was so real. I'm telling you, it's going to happen."

The next morning, I drove him to the train station. On the way back home, the accident happened exactly as in the dream. The lady walked over to my car window. "Are you hurt, honey?" she asked nervously.

When I looked up at her and realized she was the woman in my dream, I trembled. "I'm fine." But I was shaken to my core. I didn't realize I had had a precognition. I called my husband at work. "Remember my dream last night? Well, it happened."

"Don't be silly, it's just a coincidence."

After the car was fixed, we never discussed it again.

Later that year, I had a dream that ended my first marriage. My husband called from work.

"I'm going to be home late tonight Kath - meeting a few friends for drinks here in Manhattan."

"Okay, see you later."

Two o'clock in the morning, a vision interrupted my sleep. I saw him sitting next to a pretty, dark-haired woman. They were on stools nestled close to one another, whispering, giggling, drinking and smoking. That vision was as clear as if it were happening right in front of me. A wave of jealousy and anger came over me. I told myself, *it's just a dream. No need to get upset.* I put the pillow over my head and tried to get back to sleep, but the feeling was relentless. My gut felt he was in a local bar, a mile from home. Being a runner, I could easily get there in a few minutes, see if he was there and quickly run back. I'd prove to myself that I was being silly, and I'd never be suspicious again. I threw on my jacket and running shoes and ran out the door.

When I got to the bar, I peeked in the window and froze. He was in there with the brunette. The one in my vision. There they were, sitting close to one another, laughing. Anger consumed me. Without thinking, I opened the door, walked in and tapped him on the shoulder. When he turned, I belted him with a right hook to the jaw, knocking him off the stool. You could hear a pin drop as I walked out. "That must have been his wife," the bartender quipped.

There were other psychic experiences scattered throughout my life, but it wasn't until my early forties that my abilities erupted like a volcano.

Chapter 2

Perry

After my visit to Su Casa, my quest for knowledge and spiritual growth became my passion. I went to a variety of classes on topics such as tarot cards, extraterrestrials, hands-on healing, Buddhism, and Hinduism. Since there were no meet-up groups on the Internet back in the nineties, information on lectures and groups was obtained from fliers in health food stores or yoga studios. One particular flier advertised monthly gatherings with speakers on a variety of holistic topics. The next meeting was in two days.

I arrived late. Apologetically, I squeezed passed a dozen or so people in a row to find an empty seat. As I settled down, I felt a penetrating gaze. I turned around to see where it was coming from and locked eyes with a handsome man.

During the break, I went to the ladies' room. When I came out of the bathroom and walked through the lobby, he was standing in front of me, smiling. My heart pounding, I smiled graciously. He was tall and lean, with dirty blonde hair and soulful blue eyes.

"Hi. My name is Perry." His voice was enchanting. Serenity blanketed his face. He held out his hand to shake mine.

"I'm Kathy." Flushed, I scrambled for words. "It's a bit stuffy. No ventilation."

"Yes, and the topic is dull."

We talked, and time flew until the sound of clapping from inside the lecture hall caught our attention. I looked down at my watch; the presentation was over. People were leaving.

As we walked out the door, Perry said, "I really enjoyed talking with you. Would you like to go out next Saturday?"

"I'd love to."

Influenced by growing up in Brooklyn, and watching Saturday Night Fever, I wore a black mini-skirt, fitted blouse, and high-heeled shoes. Perry, far from a fashionista, donned a multi-color Hawaiian shirt, white pants, and white patent leather shoes.

At The Terrace, a nightclub in Connecticut, he swept me up in a warm embrace as if we had known each other for a lifetime. "It's so good to see you again. Let's dance." Perry grabbed my hand and ushered me to the floor.

Even though rock music was playing, he led me in a tango from one end of the dance floor to the other, weaving in and out of all the dancers. At one point, he lifted me up and swung me around like a carousel. It was different from what everyone else was doing, but it didn't seem to matter to him what people thought. Me? I was mortified because everyone was watching. After a while, I didn't care.

As dawn started to light up the morning sky, we went for breakfast at a nearby diner. It was crowded, and we had to wait a few minutes to be seated. I could smell the aroma of fresh brewed coffee, and saw that most people were having breakfast, while others were taking delight in dessert.

Once seated, we received our food order quickly. Enjoying my waffle smothered in syrup and butter, I looked at Perry. *What beautiful features he has. A perfectly sculpted nose. Deep sea blue eyes. Sandy blonde hair. A gentle and enchanting nature. The serenity yet stirring I feel in his presence.* He caught me gazing at him. Startled I stumbled to find words. "You possess a calmness that I envy."

He touched my hand and his face turned serious. "You know Kathy, I wasn't always so together. I was pretty wild when I was young. Constantly testing myself to the limit. I didn't know who I was. At that point, I quit my job and traveled to the rain forest in South America for a few months. While there, I learned to still my mind by meditating for hours at a time. I found a level of peace I didn't know existed. I survived on fruits and vegetation in the forest. I came to realize we all share a universal consciousness. We are all one. Anything that happens to one of us, affects us all." He took a sip of his coffee.

"Perry, I have never met anyone like you." I wondered, *what would it be like to kiss him?*

Finally, at around 6 am, Perry walked me to my car. I unlocked my door and before I could say anything, he took my face in his hands and passionately kissed me. My toes curled.

"Come home with me, Kathy," he whispered. He continued to kiss my face and neck sending chills down my spine. I was extremely attracted to him on every level. Part of me wanted to drop the mores of my upbringing and follow him blindly. *I've never felt like this before. Would I ever feel like this again? And the natural sweet smell of his skin. Mmm. On the other hand, how could I? It's going too fast.* I was torn and had to make an instant decision. All I managed to utter was, "I can't."

He pressed for a different answer. "Why not?"

I blurted out, "Well, because we just met!" I couldn't catch my breath. "Besides, we live two hours apart from one another."

Perry looked bewildered as his eyes searched my face. "So? What does that mean? Time should not be a factor on any level. We are attracted to one another in so many ways – spiritually, emotionally and sexually." He ran his hands down the sides of my arms eliciting goose bumps. "I can take you on a journey you've never experienced before. Kath, for once in your life be in the moment." He started dancing around with his arms moving through the air, humming to the beat of a waltz. He grabbed my hand and twirled me around.

I stopped dancing. My smile faded. "Perry, it sounds wonderful, but I can't just jump into this. You know I'm attracted to you, but I need time. Time to get to know you."

He became quiet, disappointment enshrouding his face. He planted a kiss on my cheek and opened my car door.

I got in and rolled the window down. "Talk tomorrow?"

He nodded and smiled faintly as he waved.

After that night, the electricity between us waned but we remained friends. We lived two hours apart, so our conversations were mainly by telephone.

There were times when I wondered, *did I do the right thing? Should I have cast caution to the wind and followed my heart?* I'll never know. What I did come to realize in the following weeks was that Perry came into my life for my spiritual growth and development.

One night, I sat up from my bed like a shot and watched this white ball hovering about three feet above me. I blinked a few times thinking my eyes were deceiving me. It began to spread out and slowly disintegrate. Then I saw what I can only describe as a spool of brilliant colored ribbon unravel before me. First blue, then indigo. Next, a spool of vibrant violet speedily unraveled. I couldn't process what I had just seen. *How could I tell anyone what occurred?*

In the meantime, I realized every time I spoke with Perry, I experienced the strangest things. My heart and throat vibrated for hours. It was an internal vibrating not visible to others, but it successfully kept me up at night. *Was it Perry or was I getting Parkinson's?* In a panic, I telephoned Marilyn, the psychic from Su Casa, and told her what had happened. She listened intently, then burst out laughing.

"There's nothing wrong with you, Kath. Your chakras are turning on my dear."

"My what???"

"Your chakras. There are seven main energy centers in our bodies, each associated with the meridian system, acupuncture points and the endocrine system. The lower chakras, the first four are linked with the physical plane - sex, survival and finances, feelings and love. The fifth, sixth and seventh, or the throat, third eye and crown chakras are connected to spiritual growth and development. Those are the ones tuning into a higher frequency."

"What about the colors I saw?"

"Well, the fifth chakra at the throat is blue and associated with communication and speaking your truth. The sixth chakra is indigo, between the eyebrows. It is also called the "third eye," where psychic ability resides. The last is associated with spiritual connection, understanding, and bliss - the crown chakra on the very top of the head. Some teachers say it's violet, others say it's white.

"Okay, but what does this have to do with Perry?"

"People gravitate towards people with similar vibrations

such as kids who are mischievous, or nerds hanging out with other nerds, and doctors with other doctors. Are you with me so far?"

"I think so," I responded faintly, still trying to absorb the explanation.

"Let's use the example of two tuning forks. If you strike one, a vibration and sound will emanate from that tuning fork. If a second tuning fork is in the vicinity of the first one, it will start to vibrate on the same level. Perry is one tuning fork and you are another. So, Perry's energy assisted you in reaching a higher vibration. Ultimately, this will assist you in whatever you do."

"You mean nothing is wrong with me?"

"Precisely! Just relax."

Good God. This seemed surreal. My chakras began vibrating every day and it was hard to ignore them since they interfered with my concentration.

I called Perry to tell him about my experience.

"Your vibrating chakras could be exacerbated by your resistance to it," he offered. "Don't focus on it. Focus on your awareness. Use your sensing ability. Just acknowledge the experience and let it go. My chakras were on for long lengths of time before they balanced. Awareness is not only from the eyes. Every part of the body senses, even the skin. Right now, you are learning awareness through your chakras. About 5% of consciousness is all that most of us utilize. Kathy, you are starting to tap into that 95%."

"This is a great deal of information to assimilate, Perry."

He laughed. "Yes, in the beginning it is. Just surrender to the process; otherwise, it may linger on longer than necessary. Maybe it will be easier if you look at it as a "passage," like puberty or menopause, only this is a passage to your higher self. Remember, if you weren't ready, you would not be having this experience."

I trusted Perry's advice. Within a few weeks the vibrations calmed until one day I noticed they were gone.

Chapter 3

Grandma Rose and Mom

One of the people I could talk to about developments, such as my blossoming chakras and energy, was my mother, Josephine. Although it was hard for her to believe when I told her about the beings I saw, she had an open mind because of her own intuitive experiences. One experience she had was when her brother, Danny, died at age 19. Mom had just come home from the hospital and the family did not tell her of his death for fear it would disturb her recovery. The first night, she sat up in bed and saw her brother open the closet door, take his hat and say goodbye. The next morning when she mentioned her experience, her sister Kate became unraveled and started to cry. That's when she told her that Danny died a few days earlier.

Psychic ability and the ability to heal others ran on my

mother's side of the family. My grandmother Rose who was born in 1883 worked with dreams, herbs for natural healing, and removing the "evil eye." Back in the 1950's, when I was a little tot, we lived in Brooklyn with Grandma Rose in a first-floor apartment. She only spoke Italian, so my communication with her was limited.

I don't recall much about Grandma Rose, because she died in 1956 when I was seven. One thing I do remember vividly was that she was different; she had six fingers on one hand. The sixth finger was smaller than the rest and it jutted out the side of her thumb. The doctor cut it off at birth but when it grew back they left it alone.

Grandma was a devout Catholic, always immersed in prayer with rosary beads in her hands. Her lips were constantly moving as she recited Novenas. A mini altar was assembled in her room atop a row of intricately designed hand embroidered doilies.

She had a vegetable garden with tomatoes, peppers, zucchini, eggplant, herbs and fig trees. I loved to go in the backyard and pick the ripened vegetables. But my favorite was climbing the fig trees to get the fruit. She also believed in homemade spirits - wooden barrels dotted the backyard for wine. Grandma Rose also made sure to place food scraps, egg shells and used coffee grinds around the roots of the trees and vegetable plants for nutrition.

Mom relayed stories about people who came to see grandma

for healings. Some people thought they had what is called in Italian, the "Malocchio," or "evil eye" which is a curse that someone puts on another person. Grandma Rose would sit the person down, dip her thumb in oil and make the sign of the cross three times on the person's forehead. Then she put her thumb in a bowl of water, said an incantation, and followed it by observing the configuration in the bowl to determine whether or not the person had the "Malocchio." If she determined they were cursed with the evil eye, she would repeat the process until the evil eye was gone.

Grandma Rose knew a lot about natural healing too. The knowledge that she had was passed down from generation to generation. For example, when the doctor told Grandma Rose that her son, my uncle Joe, had to have his gangrenous toe cut off, she told the doctor no, and took her son home, applied a homemade poultice and wrapped it in lettuce. Within a few weeks the toe had healed.

She used spider webs on cuts and scrapes to stop the bleeding. I thought it was pretty weird, but a few years ago, I read that spider webs have healing capabilities and are loaded with vitamin K, a blood coagulant.

When I was in my 40s, I told my mother that Grandma Rose came to me in a dream and said she had a gold chain with a medallion that should have been passed on to her.

"There was a medallion but when grandma died, I think Uncle Joe got it," mom said blankly.

"But grandma told me she wanted you to have it. She was sad it was not in your possession," I insisted.

"I believe you, but it's water under the bridge. You have to pick your battles."

Mom, born in 1910, was one of 11 children. She was second to the oldest, Katherine, who was nicknamed Kate. Back in the 1930's at age twenty-nine Kate, got seriously ill. Her ankles and legs started to swell, which the doctor said was related to either kidneys or liver. Grandma told Kate she needed to drink her own urine to regain her health. (As strange as it seems, I knew a group of people who swore by this and always drank their own urine.) Kate flatly refused, and said she'd rather die.

Grandma was distraught over Kate's stubbornness. When she needed an answer, she turned to dream work. Grandma went to bed and asked the Blessed Virgin Mary to give her a sign regarding Kate's condition. On the third night, Mary came to her with a sorrowful face. With this, grandma knew her daughter would not survive her illness. Shortly thereafter, Kate died.

Although my mother was intuitive, she had no interest in developing her clairvoyance, nor did she learn the natural healing methods practiced by my grandmother. I was sorry Grandma Rose died when I was so young because I didn't have the opportunity to learn from her. All the knowledge passed down from generation to generation was lost.

Chapter 4

Su Casa Revisited

Friday afternoon, bubbling with excitement, I packed a suitcase and drove to Su Casa straight from work. I looked forward to the friendships that were developed on my first trip, especially Marilyn. Many people were returnees - except for Lenny, a fourth-grade science teacher. Lenny had chestnut brown hair slicked back with gel. He wore thick glasses and a faded Frank Zappa tee-shirt. Lenny freely admitted he was a non-believer, but curious.

Dinner was ready at 6:30. Fillet of sole almandine, potatoes with rosemary, a mixed salad and brownies. Sesame tofu was a non-fish option. During dessert, Marilyn excused herself. "I'm going to my room and will meet up with you guys in a bit. Tonight's class is in the Rec room. See you at 8:30."

Everyone showed up promptly, eagerly awaiting the evening's events. Marilyn arrived a few minutes late, clapping her hands when she got to the front of the room. "Okay people let's get started. Everyone stand up and find a partner." The noise from chairs moving on the wooden floor was deafening. "We are going to learn how to feel each other's energy imbalances."

I paired off with the man next to me, Guy.

Marilyn began to explain what we were to do. "In each pair, pick which one of you is going to be the receiver first. The other person will be the healer."

Guy looked at me. "You go first," he nudged.

"Receivers you just stand there. Healers, and you are all healers, follow along while I demonstrate. Extend your left arm up toward the ceiling, palm up. This is where you receive healing energy coming down from the universe into your hand. Feel it travel through your body. Is everybody with me?" We nodded.

"Okay. Next, feel the receiver's energy by running your right hand about two inches from the body starting from the head slowly down to the feet. Be aware of signals from the body, such as a change in temperature or tingling sensation. When you experience a signal in an area, keep your right hand on the spot with the intention of balancing the area. If you don't second guess yourselves, you should all be able to feel and direct energy. Maybe even offer some relief." she added.

I felt silly as I ran my hand on the top of Guy's head. I was surprised when I got to the front of his face and felt heat radiating from his forehead. "Do you have a headache?"

"Yeah, I do." He stared at me while I continued scanning.

I felt an area in his leg where it seemed warmer. I felt the energy pushing against my hand. "Do you have pain here?"

"Yes. Old injury."

I was surprised that I was able to easily discern differences in the body's energy field.

Marilyn went around the room to everyone. She stopped by

us. "How are you doing?"

I shrugged my shoulders. "Okay I guess, but I don't know how I'm doing this."

"You don't have to know how it works. It's natural. The more you do it, the easier it gets. So now that you found Guy has pain, balance the area and relieve it."

"But Marilyn, how ..."

"No buts!" She waved her hand at me. "Focus your intention on what you want to do. Imagine you are channeling the energy and allow it to happen. Remember, everything is energy and intention is the driver."

Guy said, "I feel something from your hand. Like a tingling."

"Me too. I feel energy emanating into your forehead." *It's hard to believe that energy could be moved by thought.* I continued working on his forehead.

"My head is feeling better!"

Marilyn overheard Guy's comment. "Keep in mind everyone, complicated issues usually take more time. Think about it though, if in a few moments, pain can be temporarily relieved, imagine if you regularly received focused healing energy!"

Lenny walked over to Guy and me.

"I overheard Guy's headache diminished with this energy exercise," Lenny said. "I didn't feel any energy with my partner. Kath, would you check me out?"

"Sure." I scanned his body, searching for differences in

temperature or any other sensations. A strong heat was emanating from his lumbar area. "Do you have pain in your lower back?"

His eyes widened. "That's exactly where I have pain."

"I'll try and channel healing energy into the area." A few minutes elapsed. "Do you notice any change in the intensity of pain?"

"I do have a disc issue, but I have to admit, I feel some relief." Lenny did a few stretches from side to side. "Usually this is very difficult to do, but right now it's manageable."

"Okay people," Marilyn shouted. "Now switch positions. The receivers are now the healers and vice versa."

Guy scanned me from head to toe. He shook his head. "Dammit, I don't feel a thing."

"You are trying too hard," offered Marilyn. "Allow it to happen naturally - try it again."

Eyes closed, he scanned me again. "Still nothing!"

I felt bad for him. "Don't worry, with practice it'll come to you."

Chapter 5
Table Tipping

"Later, we are going to have some fun with table tipping." Marilyn announced.

"What's that?" someone asked.

"We contact spirits and ask them to spin the table." Marilyn added. "I will need eight volunteers."

I didn't think it was possible, but what the heck, I was here. I raised my hand along with seven other people.

"The more energy you folks have the better, so go to the Rec room and listen to music. I want everyone to kick up their heels and dance. The more energy we have, the better." Marilyn looked at her watch. "It's 10:15. We'll start the table tipping at 11:30. See you then."

Thirty-three people showed up. When we arrived, Marilyn was already seated. Everyone was there for the same reason: curiosity.

"Although we have eight volunteers, I need only six right now," Marilyn explained. "The other two can stand in when the others get tired." She motioned for two people to sit on the side of the room. I was one of the six to participate. "Pick one of the tables in the room, any table. The one we picked was an old, round, American colonial wooden table. It was heavy, and not easy to move. The tabletop was about two inches thick. There was one sturdy stem in the middle which held the table upright with four "feet" protruding from the bottom.

Marilyn motioned for us to stand around the table. "Now put your hands palms down barely touching the top of the table - just enough so that you know there is something under your hands. Don't put any pressure on the table," she cautioned. "We are going to chant, 'spin, table spin', over and over. At some point, you will feel the table starting to move, and then speed up. Eventually, it will begin to spin. Continue chanting, until I tell you otherwise."

Marilyn started talking to the spirits, inviting them to join us for some fun.

Then we began chanting. "Spin table spin! Spin table spin!"

"LOUDER PEOPLE! I can't hear you."

"SPIN TABLE SPIN!   SPIN TABLE SPIN!" We looked at each other not knowing what to expect. Five minutes passed. Ten. The onlookers were losing interest. Nothing seemed to be happening. My hands were getting tired hovering over the table.

Marilyn shouted, "Don't stop now folks. Be patient! Keep chanting!"

All of a sudden, the table started vibrating.

"Do you feel that?" I said looking at the others. My heart started racing.

"Yes," everyone shouted in unison.

"Holy shit! I can't believe this is happening," Lenny shouted.

We continued chanting louder. "SPIN TABLE SPIN!" A few more minutes went by and the table started moving in a circular fashion. First the table moved slowly, then sped up to the point where we had to take our right hands off the table, turn to the side, leaving our left hands barely touching the surface and walking around. It went so fast at one point, we were almost running. Excitement filled the air. We began chanting louder and louder, "SPIN TABLE SPIN." This feverish pace lasted ten minutes. We were getting tired and motioned to the other volunteers to take our places. Terrified, no one would.

The table began to slow down, and then came to a sudden halt. We looked at each other.

Marilyn said, "DON'T move your hands. Stay where you are."

Within a minute, the table slowly began to go in reverse. After a few minutes, it tipped over and fell. I expected to hear a crashing sound but there was none.

Lenny was standing where the table fell. "Jeez. Did you see that? I watched the table fall, felt movement of air, but there was no noise." His face was white as a ghost. "Did we really do that with our minds?" He scratched his head. "It doesn't make sense."

"I agree. It defies logic."

"Yeah, but Marilyn also said spirits manifested energy to move the table," Mary chimed in.

"Maybe there was a synergism of energy between our minds and spirits," I offered. *A lot of things aren't making sense lately, but I find it intoxicating.* "Whatever it was, it blew my mind."

The weekend flew by quickly. Sunday afternoon and it was time to leave. Marilyn and I embraced. "I'm so glad you came up Kath. You are my best student." Our eyes locked. "And, you are a healer."

As those words penetrated my brain, I froze. *My God, I've been hearing that in my head for the past few months.* Tears filled my eyes. I took a deep breath and regained my composure. "Marilyn, shortly before my first trip to Su Casa, I began hearing a voice. Sometimes in the evening before going to sleep, other times while driving, or reading. I didn't know why, or where it was coming from. I thought I was losing my sanity. How could I tell anyone? People who hear voices are crazy. I thought the stress and strain of coping with my daughter's illness, had finally put me over the edge. Now, the voice makes sense."

"I'm glad I could allay your fear," Marilyn said with confidence. "You have the opportunity to help people heal."

"You said everyone is a healer," I countered.

"Yes, everyone has healing abilities, but some more than others. Besides, you love helping people. Hands-on healing is a non-conventional method, but I believe it will become more widely acceptable." She smiled. "Kathy, even though you have these abilities, it's good to have some kind of credentials. Get training in energy work, such as Reiki. It will help focus and refine your abilities."

"Why didn't you tell me I was a healer the first time we met?"

"You weren't ready to hear it. You had to learn other things first. You had to crawl before you could walk."

Tears of joy streamed down my face. All those months of hearing a voice led up to this moment. I felt relieved. *I wasn't going crazy.*

Chapter 6

Meditation

My first experience with Transcendental Meditation (TM) was in the early 1970's. The Maharishi Yogi introduced TM to the West and was spiritual guru to celebrities including the Beatles. Instead of the familiar universal mantra, *Om*, with TM we were given our own sacred sound. The mantra was typically melodious and helped create a spiritual space for meditation. There was training on the basic concepts of TM along with a great deal of practice. Every weekend I trekked into Manhattan for practice and training. We were guided to close our eyes, relax with gentle breathing and focus on our mantra. If thoughts came into mind, they were to be acknowledged and allowed to softly dissipate.

Although at first the practice seemed excruciatingly mundane, the benefits were immeasurable. I welcomed the sense of clarity, focus, vibrant energy, and overall feeling of peace. Even though I believe TM helped me to maintain a normal blood pressure for years while high blood pressure ran in my family, it wasn't until I experienced the presence of beings at Su Casa that my meditations became incredibly deep. I sensed them trying to communicate with me and reached out to them in my mind's eye, but only received the transmission of brilliant colors. I felt they were trying to tune into a compatible frequency.

One day in meditation, we finally connected telepathically. First came bright colors which morphed into crisp images. They showed me plant and animal life from their galaxy. The information came through as if slides were being shown in my mind, vivid and clear but like a silent movie - no words.

Then something strange happened. Like in a Stephen King movie, I had the feeling of a presence in the room. I came out of my meditation and glanced around the room. I didn't see anything, but my arms were a mass of gooseflesh. *Was I being watched?*

I walked to the bathroom and instinctively slammed the door shut and threw my body against it. *Why did I do that? I live alone.* Slowly, I opened the door and peeked out. No one was there. I dismissed the feeling.

Later that evening, I turned the light off and lay down in bed. The same feeling I felt in the bathroom arose throughout my body. I shuddered. *I am being watched.* I jolted up in bed and struggled for the light. I looked around the room. *I don't SEE anyone, but I FEEL them.* My heart was pounding out of my chest. Then I began to see them with my third eye. They were hovering around, observing me. I was petrified. I propped up my pillow and watched them, too terrified to sleep. *I have to stay awake, so they don't try inhabit my body or take me away*. I must have dozed off because the next morning, I opened my eyes, squinting from the light. Exhausted, I tried to convince myself it was a nightmare, but as I became lucid, once again I felt their presence.

What am I going to do? I can't call the police. They would take me to the crisis unit for a mental evaluation. I can't tell anyone. Jeez, who would believe me?

So I did nothing. Interestingly enough, they didn't follow me to work. They stayed in my home and observed me in the shower, getting dressed, eating and sleeping. I could feel the adrenaline coursing through my body, and intermittent cold sweats. I could barely eat. The only time I felt relief, was when I was out of the house.

Every day, I dreaded going home. At night, I kept vigil with the light on and eyes open. I felt some control by staying awake as long as I could. I thought if I fell into a deep sleep they would seize control. From sheer exhaustion, every night I fell into light sleep. Every morning my body felt as though it had had the crap kicked out of it. *How much longer could I take this without losing my mind?*

Finally, after two weeks, I was so tired and irritable, I got angry. Really furious. I started pacing the floor, flailing my arms about, stamping my feet screaming, "I've had enough! What do you want from me? I'm tired of having you around. Get the hell out of my house!" Tears ran down my face. "You've invaded my privacy long enough! I haven't been able to sleep. I don't care if you want to contact me. Go find someone else. I NEVER want to be contacted again! GET OUT! GET THE F--- OUT!" I felt the veins in my neck pop.

When I came to my senses, I wondered, *Are they angry now? Are there consequences?* I held my breath and looked around. I couldn't sense them, even when I closed my eyes. *My God, they are gone.*

That evening I felt confident enough to turn the light off. *No one watching me. I'm alone.* I curled up under the sheets, my body molded into the mattress. I slept like a baby for the first time in weeks.

Chapter 7

The Shekinah Fire

Just when I thought things had quieted down, I walked into a bookstore, and noticed a man behind the counter talking to a customer. He caught my gaze and our eyes locked. At that moment, his body was surrounded by a white glow, and his voice had an unusual vibrational tone as though I was hearing his voice in an echo chamber.

I couldn't hear or see anyone else in the store. It seemed like there was just the two of us, connected by a tunnel of white energy. I started sweating and said, "Gee it's awfully warm in here," as I fanned myself with my hand and pushed the hair off the sides of my face.

The man laughed. "I'm the store manager, Archie. Now I

know you are going to find this hard to believe, but it's really not warm in here. You see, you are experiencing the Shekinah Fire. When Christ told people not to touch him it wasn't because he shunned them, but at that moment they would have burned up from the heat of his aura."

Okay, I said to myself. *This guy is a nut! I need to get my ass out of here!* I smiled graciously, made my purchase, and left. By the time I got to my car, I was on fire. I glanced in the rear-view mirror. Beads of sweat dotted my forehead and upper lip. My ears and face were flushed. Then a strong wave of heat blazed up my spine. *What the heck is going on?*

I rushed home, ran to the medicine cabinet and shoved the thermometer in my mouth, expecting a fever. Two minutes later the thermometer registered 98.6. Normal.

Could this have something to do with the strange man I had just met? Embarrassed, I called the store and relayed the occurrence to Archie.

"If you come back to the store, I'll explain."

With that, I jumped into my car.

When I got there, he smiled and waved me over to the seat next to him. "You are probably going to find this explanation really strange but stay with me. You have felt the Shekinah fire or the presence of God. A person feels the glow, then the fire burning, and finally, His presence." He stopped talking to ring up a customer. "Few people feel it. Some don't know what they are feeling, so, they don't pay attention to it. You, my friend, knew it was special."

"I wouldn't exactly say that, it just felt really strange." Thinking it was a one-time occurrence, the next day at work I felt feverish again and ran to the nurse's office to have her take my temperature. It was normal. Every day for a week, the same thing occurred. Intense warmth in my spine and face, but no fever. To avoid an awkward situation, I brought a thermometer to work and took my temperature in a bathroom stall. I called Archie.

"Kathy, the energy will balance out after a while. This phenomenon is the rising of the Kundalini energy. Kundalini originally from Sanskrit, an ancient language of India, is a spiritual fire or energy that has different names in each religion. The fire is awakened in us to purify our bodies and raise our consciousness. The awakening of Kundalini should be done slow, with the help of a master. Your experience was instantaneous. Just be patient."

Experiences including ET contact, opening chakras, Kundalini, and the force behind the table spinning seemed totally different, yet they had a common factor: a powerful unseen energy.

Looking back, I know that Archie along with Perry and Marilyn and other people I encountered in my life were instrumental in my accessing various energies. Each one of them had a part in creating a work of art. Orchestrating a fine piece of music.

A door beyond the physical world had opened up, and I was walking through it.

Part II: Receiving and Transmitting Energy

Chapter 8

UFO's

Penny had jet black hair pulled back into a ponytail. She wore eyeliner that tapered off into a thin tail at the end of each eye, high heels lengthened her short stature. Penny's smile was captivating with a back drop of bright red lipstick. "How many people here have had some kind of encounter?"

I was afraid to raise my hand, but when I looked around the conference room, everyone had their hands up. I quickly raised mine.

"That's great," the speaker said, stroking her chin thoughtfully. "So glad you could all be here tonight. My name is Penny Stiller."

"I'll start by sharing my personal story which took place in the early 1980's. I was driving on the Palisades Interstate Parkway in Rockland County, New York. A disk-shaped flying saucer suddenly appeared overhead. Beams of bright lights lit up the car and the road."

My God, I thought. *Hearing this makes me realize I'm not the only one who has had extraterrestrial experiences.*

"It was so close, I thought it was going to land on the parkway. Reflex made me and the cars behind me, hit the brakes." She made slapping sounds with her hands. "Luckily, we didn't wind up in an accident."

"You must have been terrified," someone yelled from the

back of the room.

"Beyond terrified. The UFO stood still hovering over us. I had to shield my eyes from the blinding light. Thoughts flashed through my mind of being carted away and experimented on." Penny paused for a moment. "I was relieved when in a matter of seconds, it zoomed away. But my heart was still pounding, and it took a few minutes to catch my breath."

Talking about her encounter, produced visible anxiety, but she quickly recovered.

"After that, I joined the National Investigations Committee on UFOs (NICUFO), founded in 1967 by Dr. Frank E. Stranges, who wrote, *The Stranger at the Pentagon* and *Strangers from the Pentagon: The UFO Conspiracy.*

Penny took a sip of water. "Allegedly, all of the astronauts saw UFOs while in space, but were sworn to secrecy. Since you all had some kind of encounter, you may know they fall into five categories - from a sighting, to direct contact. Have any of you seen the movie *Communion*?" Heads nodded.

"That was direct contact, communication with aliens. They are usually seen in the house at night and are called 'bedroom visitors.'"

Feeling more at ease, I raised my hand. "The beings I saw were dark blue."

"The blues are Star Warriors, small of stature with translucent skin and large almond shaped eyes. Mediums who communicate psychically with them, have claimed that they won't harm us. Their message to humanity is "'pursue your passion'" and "'do not allow yourself to be pressured into being anything but who you are.'"

I was relieved to hear they were non-aggressive in nature.

"There are many different species. Some are here to help, like the ones you saw." Penny looked at me. "Then there are the grays, whose images are splashed on tabloids. They are usually connected to stories of kidnapping for experimentation."

Penny took out some pictures of aliens and spread them out on the table in front of the room. "In the eighties, Rockland County and the entire Hudson Valley area were a hot-bed for UFOs."

The floor was open to the audience who shared their personal stories. Some saw UFOs, others came face-to-face with ETs. One woman said she was kidnapped, endured painful experimentation and was returned. Another said he had implants under his skin. Most people had sightings.

Penny expressed concerns that some of us might be contacted again. She searched through piles of copies. She found what she was looking for and plopped a bunch of papers in front of the first person seated.

"Take one and pass on the rest. This prayer, *The Ring of Fire*, should be said every night; it will keep you safe," she said reassuringly. "During sleep, you are most vulnerable. Also, whenever you sense their presence, imagine yourself enclosed in a blue light - the Ring of Fire."

After the lecture, I approached the woman who had night-time visitors in her home. When did your encounter occur?"

"In the summer of 1991. Late August, I'd say."

I got the chills. *My God, that was the same time of my visitation. My encounters were not just in my head. They were real.* How many people in Rockland and the entire Hudson Valley had contact but were afraid to discuss their experiences with anyone?

Chapter 9

Dr. Gilda

Linda and I were having lunch at my favorite restaurant. Only a few weeks earlier, we met at a meditation session in Nyack, New York, but became fast friends. Linda was a tall, willowy woman with long, silky blonde hair. I was drawn to her peaceful demeanor and gentle voice. As we chatted, I realized we had much in common. Then out of the blue she asked, "Do you know what channeling is?"

"Yes. Communication between humans, angelic beings, and other non-physical entities. My friend Marilyn allows a spirit or entity to use her body to speak through her."

"Great. I'm with a small group of people who are learning to channel. Would you like to join us?"

"The thought hasn't crossed my mind. Sounds intriguing."

"My friends and I have been driving to Pennsylvania the last few Saturdays for training with our teacher, Dr. Gilda, a retired medical doctor. She teaches students to channel different entities from the non-physical world." Linda put her hand on my shoulder. "I think you will fit right in. Why don't you join us?"

When Saturday came, Linda, and her two friends, Jason and Melanie, met me at 8 am in front of the local health food store for the trip.

When I first walked into Dr. Gilda's apartment, I became dizzy and disoriented. It felt like I had high altitude sickness.

I leaned over and whispered to Linda. "All of a sudden I feel sick, but in a strange way. I hear talking but it sounds like I'm listening through a bottle and looking through a dense fog."

"It's the energy in the room," she murmured. "Don't worry, your body will settle down and balance itself out. You'll be fine." She patted my hand. It took about an hour for me to feel connected to my body again.

We were seated in a circle as Dr. Gilda explained. "We are meeting here for a purpose, all from the same distant galaxy, finally reunited." She turned to me. "Welcome to our family, a reunion of souls from a distant past."

This feels strange, like an episode from the X-Files. I smiled weakly.

She continued, "In time, each and every one of you will be channeling someone." She took a few moments to study the energy around each person. "Jason, you will be channeling archangels, Melanie, the Blessed Virgin Mary will be coming through you. Linda, John the Baptist." She turned to me. "You, Kathy, will channel ETs."

OMG! My stomach became queasy as my mind raced back to the alien contact at Su Casa and my home. I was deep in thought when Dr. Gilda's voice pulled me out of it.

"Kathy are you ok?"

I didn't want to tell the group how scared I was. "Yeah. I'm fine."

"Good. Right now, I'm going to clear out everyone's chakras one by one," Dr. Gilda announced. She motioned for one of us to volunteer to go first. Jason jumped up and sat in the designated chair. "Since Kathy is new, I will explain what I'm doing." She began working. "First, energetically, I am removing Jason's esoteric body from his physical body, cleaning it, and putting it back."

Everyone else claimed they could see what Dr. Gilda was doing. I couldn't see anything. They assured me that at first, they didn't either.

It was my turn to sit in what was fondly called, the "hot seat." I didn't know what to expect, but immediately felt the movement of energy through my body.

"You have some heavy energy I wouldn't be able to clear out now in front of the group - because it would take time to remove," she announced. "I suggest you come back for a private session."

I was unnerved by her suggestion until I learned everyone else had heavy energy when they first started. Throughout the day, Dr. Gilda led us in and out of meditation a half dozen times. With each meditation, I went in deeper and deeper, which made it harder to return. I wanted to stay in such a peaceful and serene place.

The day sped by, and as we were leaving, I happened to mention I was beginning Reiki training the following week.

"You should get an individual clearing session beforehand," Dr. Gilda suggested.

"Why?"

"As I mentioned before, it will clean out heavy energy and tune up the body and mind so you are more receptive to your training."

Filled with anxiety, I booked an individual session on Wednesday.

When I arrived, a short buxom woman greeted me at the door. "Hi, I'm Maia, her assistant. So good to meet you," she said, as she gave me a warm hug. "Follow me."

"Aha, here is our newest protégé." She patted the folding chair between them. "Come sit here." She touched the side of my arm. "Just so you know, Kathy, I call on Jesus to help. Is that comfortable for you?"

"It's fine. I was brought up Catholic. I'm just surprised that you call on an official religious figure."

"Spirituality and religion don't necessarily have to stand apart. One doesn't negate the other. My beliefs, your beliefs - they are all very individual."

"When you put it that way, it makes sense."

"Good." She closed her eyes and beckoned her spirit guides. Within a few minutes, she began to speak. "In the name of Jesus, I command any negative entities to leave Kathy's body." She made motions with her hands, pulling energy away from my body. She continued with incantations, and at one point, I didn't know if it was real or my imagination, I saw a dark image pop out of my body. I watched it float away. At that point, I said to myself, *this is real.*

Next, she used incense while she led me into a meditative state. My eyes were closed when I saw a woman. As the image became clearer, I realized it was my Aunt Kate. Although I never met her because she died in the 1920's, many years before I was born, I had seen pictures. She was tall and slender, and her blouse was neatly dressed with an elegant bow. Mom had told me she played the violin and had a melodic soprano voice. "Though she wasn't worldly, Kate seemed to know the right thing to do," mom used to say. "She was the oldest of the siblings and watched over all of us like a hawk, making sure we didn't get into trouble."

I have always felt Aunt Kate's presence around me. Maybe it was because she was the family protector. At the precise moment I saw Aunt Kate in twenties attire, Dr. Gilda snapped me out of my reverie with a question.

"Who is the young woman here with us, dressed in 1920's clothing?"

I got the chills. This was validation Aunt Kate was close at hand. It wasn't my imagination playing tricks on me because Dr. Gilda saw her too. "She's my Aunt Kate."

The clearing took two hours. Dr. Gilda said she saw a great deal of negative energy leaving my body. I felt dynamic movement, especially from the top of my head, where the energy exited.

"Finally," she said, "Kathy you are all cleared. The Reiki training will be more effective now."

"Thanks Dr. Gilda. I'm looking forward to the training. It's going to be at my house." Once again, she had a troubled look on her face.

"Try to have it somewhere else."

I saw her uneasiness. "Why?"

"If all the people go to your house for Reiki training, they will release a great deal of pain, and negative energy, which would stay in the house."

I shuddered at the thought. "It's too late to change arrangements, the teacher is coming from Colorado," I said weakly. "Her plane tickets were bought months ago, and everything was paid in advance." I was shaken and, my thoughts were racing. "Maybe someone else could have it in their house. I'll call everyone as soon as I get home."

Dr. Gilda saw my distress. "That's a good idea. Don't worry though, if you must have it at your house, I'll help you clear it."

When I got home, I called Suzie, one of the people who was coming for the training and told her what happened.

"You can't back out now! You are the only one who has a quiet house without a husband and children. You offered. You must have it there," she insisted.

"I know, I know," I countered, "but that was before I knew everyone would be discharging their negative stuff in my house."

"Well, I'll ask around, but I think you should get hold of yourself and reconsider," she snapped and hung up the phone.

Reiki training was only a few days away, and I was falling apart. I called my mentor, Marilyn.

"Kathy, haven't you listened to anything I taught you?" she scolded. "Nothing can hurt you. Your energy is powerful, and you are working out of love, so how can this be bad? Forget what Dr. Gilda said. I'm telling you, it will be fine."

I hung up the phone. Still unnerved, I called the Reiki Master in Colorado. She listened patiently before she replied.

"I will be clearing your house before and after each day's work, so you don't have anything to worry about. Besides, with the Reiki training you are going to be taught powerful Japanese symbols and will be able to clear your own house."

I breathed a sigh of relief.

Chapter 10

Reiki Training

For the three days before the Reiki training, we were advised to eliminate animal protein, caffeine, alcohol, sugar, cigarettes as well as limit negative distractions such as violent movies. I struggled with the protein and caffeine restrictions but muddled through with lots of peanut butter and the decaffeinated drink of the era, Sanka.

It was difficult to contain my excitement as I awaited the arrival of Anna, the Reiki Master. She was trained in China but born in the USA. Our only contact was by phone so when she arrived, I expected to see a diminutive Asian woman. Instead, when I opened the door I was surprised to find Anna: 5'6", of Italian descent, mid-thirties, wearing blue jeans, a tee shirt and sneakers.

She twirled her russet-brown hair into a makeshift bun and addressed the group. "We have a lot of work to do. The training is intense consisting of lectures, meditations, attunements, and practicing Reiki on one another. Let's get started."

After some discussion and a meditation, the six of us received our first Reiki attunement. Anna energetically placed the first healing Reiki symbol through the top of our heads. Next she showed us the hand placements to be used when performing a balancing and healing. We paired off and took turns working on each other. In the middle of our second meditation, Anna said, "Now that you are in a place of comfort and peace, ask your Reiki guide to reveal him or herself to you."

This is hogwash! I thought to myself. *I don't believe anyone will come to me. Kath, calm down and go along with it.* In the split second I acquiesced, a Native American appeared in my mind's eye with a leathered face, wearing a full headdress. He stood there, tall and proud, and began to speak. "My name is Shin Wa or White Eagle. I am a shaman. A medicine man." *Was this my imagination or was this real?* My thoughts were interrupted when Anna brought us out of the meditation. We sat there looking at one another, but no one discussed their experience. "Anna is it all right for us to disclose our Reiki guides?"

"Sure."

One of the initiates described her guide as a short, bald man. Another saw a plain, nondescript looking woman. Everyone said they saw and sensed their guides. I noticed no one else had an auditory experience.

I was the last one to speak. "My guide said his name was White Eagle." I expected everyone to laugh.

"There is a White Eagle," Anna replied. Her response gave me the fortitude to continue.

"He said he was a shaman or medicine man."

"White Eagle is a shaman," she assured me, "and there is a person who claims to channel White Eagle."

My God! There is a White Eagle. What amazing energy am I tapping into?

At each level of training, we received stronger symbols. I didn't feel any different, but something had changed. I looked around the room at my fellow initiates. They looked completely relaxed and at peace. Their eyes were aglow. The change was emanating from the inside out.

We were taught the Reiki principles. Although simple in theory, they were challenging to follow.

Just for today, do not worry.
Just for today, do not anger.
Honor your parents, teachers and elders.
Earn your living honestly.
Show gratitude to every living thing.

After the Master attunement, Anna conducted the closing ceremony, which I found to be a powerful and humbling experience. Three of us were instructed to sit in chairs while the other three stood facing each seated person. All were barefoot. The people standing were asked to kneel in front of the three who were seated. A basin with olive oil was handed to the kneelers who were asked to wash the person's feet in front of them with the oil while saying, "Please allow me to serve myself by serving you."

Then the seated people and kneelers switched, and the ceremony was repeated. After that, Anna knelt in front of each one of us, washing our feet with oil, saying, "Please allow me to serve myself by serving you." Then she kissed each person's feet. "Thank you for being my teacher," she added as she looked into each person's eyes.

I felt a dramatic shift in my consciousness. The energy of my heart expanded in a way I never felt before, overflowing with love and gratitude. *This is what bliss must feel like.* I was floating in a sea of love. Our teacher demonstrated she was a humble servant of a higher power, just like us. The experience was a gift. An honor.

Chapter 11

Amy

After Reiki training, I offered students and faculty free ten-minute energy clearing and balancing sessions at a local college health fair. It was an opportunity to acquire practice feeling and discerning energy as well as dispense healing energy.

The Fair was from 10 am to 2 pm in the Gym. Each modality was separated by movable partitions with signs. Mine read, **Experience Reiki.** The others included nutrition, dental hygiene, blood pressure screenings, and pulmonary tests. As soon as my massage table was set up, a line began to form.

I gave an introduction to Reiki healing. "Physical ailments oftentimes start on the unseen energetic level. I am offering these mini-sessions so that people can experience energy work. It's helpful to know that there are other modalities available to aid in healing besides conventional treatments. Reiki can be used on its own or as an adjunct to traditional healing. For instance, if someone was being treated for cancer, I would not expect them to give up chemo or radiation."

"All you have to do when you are on the table is relax. I will run my hands about an inch over your body from head to toe without touching you. If I feel an imbalance, I will gently place my hands on that area and send healing energy."

A student on line had a question. "Will I feel anything?"

"You may feel some warmth, coolness, or tingling. The energy flows even if you don't feel anything."

I motioned for the first person, a young blonde girl, to come forward and lie on the table. I spent about ten minutes on each person. Some people felt a movement of energy, some didn't, but all said they felt relaxed. I was able to discern energies of ailments such as headaches, backaches, old injuries, surgeries, and women who were menstruating or in mid cycle. By 2 pm, my energy was waning. I was ready to pack up and leave. I picked my pocketbook up from under the table. As I turned around a faculty member came toward me.

"Hi I'm Amy. I teach here at the college. I stopped by earlier and watched you work on people, but I had to run to teach a class. I'd love to experience Reiki. Are you still available?"

I was tired, but I couldn't say no. "Sure. Let's get started." I pointed to the massage table. "Why don't you lie down on the table and I will scan your body." I had my hands positioned at her head and I slowly moved them along her body, feeling for any aberrations in her energy field. Over her right kidney, I felt an overwhelming sense of weight or pain radiating through my hand. Her forehead wrinkled as she looked up waiting for an explanation. "I can't seem to get past the feeling of extreme heaviness in your kidney. Did something happen here?" My hand rested on her kidney area.

"I can't believe you can feel that. I was involved in a sledding accident twenty years ago. Critically injured. I lost my left kidney. My body has recovered and adapted. I'm okay, but my right kidney has to work harder which is probably what you are feeling."

"I also sense a female who is around you at all times. She is not in the body, but in spirit."

"Oh my God, that must be my friend, Sally." She started to cry, neither one of us paying attention to the crowd that formed around us. "She was killed in the accident. I have always wondered if Sally has been with me. I carry so much guilt around because I survived the accident and she didn't." Amy wiped her tears with her fingers.

"I'm so sorry. I'm sure she wants you to let go of the guilt and be happy."

She seemed to be considering that possibility.

After a minute her eyes brightened. "I can't thank you enough for this. I feel like a dark cloud has been lifted."

"Amy, I feel blessed to be able to participate in your healing." There is something special about helping someone to alleviate a heavy heart.

Chapter 12

Danielle

After the college health fair, one of my first Reiki clients was Danielle, a woman in her twenties, wearing washed out jeans and a tight-fitting tee shirt that accentuated her flat stomach. She was visibly nervous, clenching her hands and tapping her foot. "I recently broke up with my boyfriend and I'm looking for another job. And in general, I feel a sense of malaise."

"That's understandable since those are two major areas in your life. I know it's really hard, but it helps if you just allow it to be. Accept it in this moment. That will free up some energy that is being used right now for resistance."

I could see she was mulling over what I had said. At that moment, a picture of one of her past lives flashed in my mind. "Danielle, I am getting a vision of you as an older, robust-looking gypsy in the open plains. You were a matriarch sitting around the fire with your "band." Your hair is thick and dark with bangle bracelets lining both wrists. You are shrewd because you have to ensure the survival of your band."

"The hair on my arms rose," Danielle said. "This supports what I always felt. I love to dance and especially gypsy dances, feeling the music and pirouetting around the house." Her arms were twirling and swaying as she spoke, a smile blanketing her face. "The last few years at Halloween, I even dressed up as a gypsy."

"I'm glad it makes sense to you." I motioned for her to lie down on the massage table. "I'm going to scan you by moving my hands a few inches above your body."

After a few minutes, I offered my findings. "I feel an intense heat in your legs, abdomen, your ovaries, and an energy block in your heart area. Now I'm going to direct energy into those areas. Just relax."

Danielle closed her eyes. "I feel warmth radiating through my body."

"Good. That's normal."

When my hands hovered over her ovaries, she said, "I can feel that. It feels like energy is being pulled up and out."

"That's what is happening. The process is working," I continued to scan and transmit energy. "I feel a heaviness in your stomach. Do you drink a lot of caffeine?"

"Six cups of espresso a day."

"Wow! That's a lot. I would be frazzled. How about juices?"

"Mostly orange juice."

"Can you cut down on the coffee and juice? Try to substitute with some herbal tea. It would be significantly better for you."

She nodded sheepishly. "I know my diet needs improvement."

While I continued scanning and balancing her body, I heard a man's name. "Who is Mike or Mikey? I keep hearing this name."

Danielle's eyes widened. "He's a spirit who comes to me and gives me comfort. I talk to him before I go to sleep at night."

"Oh. And who is the man who jumped or fell from a building?"

She shot me a look of surprise. "My great grandfather. Before I was born, he died falling off a building."

"I feel that he is watching over you."

"Thank you. That gives me a sense of comfort."

The session lasted one hour. "Danielle, when you go home, it is helpful to take a warm bath with one cup of apple cider vinegar."

"Isn't vinegar acidic?"

"Lemons, limes and apple cider vinegar are acidic but when consumed can alkalinize the body - vinegar in the bath helps with the detoxification process."

Danielle called the next day to say she took the prescribed bath and was so relaxed she slept like a baby. A week later, Danielle came for another appointment. She looked more relaxed.

"I have to tell you, I just got my period and this was the first time in years that I had no pain. It was the easiest one I've ever had!"

Once I started working on Danielle, I could feel the difference in her energy. It was calm and flowing nicely. Toward the end of the session, I felt the presence of two people in her energy field. "Do you know a brother and sister who died?"

"No." She seemed sure.

"There is a brother and sister here," I insisted. "I also see a street light and headlights. The light is blinding."

I continued working and a few minutes later Danielle burst out, "I know who that is! Oh my God! Johnny and his sister. They died in a car crash. He hit a street light."

"They are telling me they miss you."

"I hadn't thought about them in a long time. They were good friends." Her eyes welled. "I miss them too."

Chapter 13

Brenda

Over lunch, Brenda and I were discussing her wrist pain. She worked as an interpreter for the deaf. From constantly using her hands to produce sign language, she had developed persistent sharp numbing pains in her left forearm and wrist.

"The pain interferes with my performance," Brenda complained. I wear a wrist brace while working, which helps me to continue interpreting but it's not getting better. I know you work with energy and thought maybe you could help."

"Let me take a look." I motioned for Brenda to lift her arm towards me. I held my hand an inch above her skin. "I'm scanning your wrist. Pain has a certain energy to it, a sensation I can feel. Sometimes, it runs a little hotter than the surrounding area. Then I track the origination of the pain and channel a healing signal into the area."

Brenda had a surprised expression on her face. "This is really weird. I feel a warm tingly sensation where the pain is."

"That feeling is an acknowledgement from your body that the energy is being transmitted." I continued working. When she no longer felt any sensation, that was my signal the energy delivery had ended. "The energy will keep working over the next few days."

A week later Brenda called. "I am thrilled to tell you I have no pain. I'm not even wearing my wrist brace. Thank you, Kathy, from the tips of my fingers to the forearm of my left arm."

After the initial six months, she periodically experienced tinges of pain, but nothing like her prior discomfort.

Chapter 14

Reconnecting with White Eagle

A month after the Reiki training, White Eagle made a long-awaited appearance while I was meditating. As if watching a movie, in my mind's eye, I saw myself walking down a green-covered mountain into a valley. I was male, Native American, with leather leggings and no cloth or adornments covering my chest and back. My hair was long, straight and black. Out in the distance, I saw White Eagle approaching on a white and brown pony. My heart raced with joy. He looked magnificent in a full Native American headdress, with feathers streaming down his back. He dismounted, and I walked over to greet him. After a moment, we walked to a teepee. The flap on the teepee had two sets of brown hide, each consisting of three sets of diamond shapes overlapping one another. White Eagle held the flap open and motioned for me to go inside. As soon as we were seated, he began to smoke a pipe. "The pipe is a link between earth and sky. It is a bridge between people and nations. Now, it is a bond between White Eagle and White Rain." He handed me the pipe.

After a period of silence, he spoke. "White rain covers the earth in a blanket of white. Fresh, new, and pure. From now on, I will call you White Rain."

It must be the name they used for snow, I thought to myself.

"You must remember the power of herbs and plants; more importantly, the power of the unseen, the Great Spirit in the skies." He looked upward with his arms outstretched. "And, you must always remember patience, peace, and prayer." Then he bowed his head and again fell silent.

I basked in the field of energy surrounding us. I saw a vibrant green beam of light going through my body, encompassing each and every cell. I felt unparalleled joy.

Time passed until his voice interrupted my elation. "You are being given healing powers by the Great White Spirit which will help you heal others." At that moment, I heard the flap on the teepee open and a woman entered carrying maize. The aroma of the roasted corn awakened my sense of smell. She motioned for me to take some from the bowl.

Eager to learn from White Eagle, I quickly ate and asked a question. "White Eagle do you know what I could do for a digestion problem?" I pointed to my stomach.

He thought for a moment. "Make a tea of chamomile, bullwort, and licorice. Chew on mint leaves." Then he lowered his head and the scene began to fade.

No! No! Don't go. I have so much more to learn! And as quickly as he appeared, White Eagle was gone.

Later that day, I researched bullwort and found it was also called bishop's weed and is in the parsley family. I was amazed to find it is used to treat digestive disorders, asthma as well as applied topically for skin conditions. Chamomile is used to calm anxiety and settle the stomach while mint is soothing to the digestive tract, reducing symptoms of irritable bowel syndrome and helping to eliminate toxins from the body. Heartburn and other maladies were helped with licorice.

When I shared White Eagle's appearance with my meditation group, one of the women told me she read books on White Eagle. She said Mrs. Grace Cooke was a medium who claimed the spiritual teachings were channeled to her from her spirit guide, White Eagle.

I could barely contain my excitement. The following day I went to the metaphysical bookstore in town and found *Heal Yourself* by White Eagle. It was a short, inspirational book which motivated me to try to contact White Eagle every day in meditation. "Where are you White Eagle? Speak to me." Nothing. Disappointed, I gave up.

Unexpectedly, two weeks later during bridge pose in yoga, White Eagle appeared. As soon as I saw him, I lay down on the mat, shut my eyes, took a deep breath and relaxed completely. There he was, in my mind's eye, standing there. He looked old and wrinkled, wearing a full headdress, and a brown hide loincloth. He was facing a young woman. I could not see her face, just her bare back with thick flowing, straight, black hair.

She knelt before him as he leaned over throwing sand on her back. Once, twice, three times, until her back was covered with sand. He was performing some kind of ceremony. He pointed to his left, east. He bowed his head and prayed silently. When he was ready, he signaled for the young woman to stand up. She bowed her head in reverence, turned, and slowly walked away.

White Eagle lifted his arms in front of him with palms toward the sky. His left hand then opened up and circled the other hand. Then his right hand dipped into an image, sort of a hologram of an ocean the size of a small fishbowl and pulled out an old parchment paper. More hand movements followed; I was mesmerized.

Next, an old, Native American woman with long gray hair walked slowly from the west carrying a thin staff. She stopped for a moment, her eyes locked with White Eagle. They spoke but I could not understand what they said. She continued to walk east, until the picture faded.

Why was White Eagle showing me rituals? Could he be reminding me of the things I learned when I was his student, White Rain? Perhaps he was even reminiscing about our time together.

Chapter 15

Millie

Shopping in the health food store, a flier pinned to the corkboard caught my eye. Millie, a healer, and graduate of the Barbara Brennan School of Healing was giving a lecture and demonstration on Saturday. I had heard of Barbara Brennan, a well-known healer who wrote the book *Hands of Light*.

When I arrived at the lecture, Millie was setting up her books and massage table in front of the room. She was a pleasant-looking woman in her mid-forties with long, thick brown hair and deep brown eyes. She began her talk by explaining subtle energies and chakras. After fifteen minutes into the lecture, she asked for a volunteer. A woman in her fifties stood up and proceeded to the front of the room.

Millie asked her to lie on the massage table, then began cleaning and balancing her chakras by moving her hands in a sweeping motion. As I sat on the floor looking at the woman lying there, I saw something protruding out of the energy surrounding her heart. I couldn't identify it but wanted to know what it was. "Millie, I see this bent tubular thing hanging out over her heart, what is it?"

"That's her heart chakra."

"But it's all bent and hanging." No one else seemed to notice.

"That's because it needs to be fixed. I'm working on it now." She continued sweeping and removing energy. "Do you see anything else?"

"I notice a thin white layer of energy outlining the woman's whole body. I don't see any breaks or spikes of energy, so I'm assuming it's intact."

"Good observation. If she had dark areas, that usually signifies illness on the etheric level, an energy level surrounding the body. Illness starts there before it manifests on the physical level."

Amazed with her abilities, I wanted to feel her healing energy and proceeded to book an individual session.

When I arrived at her office, Millie asked me questions about my health and history. I mentioned my back pain. She motioned for me to lie down on the massage table and covered me with a thick soft blanket. As soon as she started working on me, I felt strong movement of energy. I watched her hands pulling energy away from me. As she pulled, she breathed in; as she shook the energy off her hands, she breathed out. She wasn't actually touching my skin but hovering a few inches above it. She was using the power of her mind and breath to orchestrate the process. I felt magnetized to the table.

"When you were a child you saw visions of Mary," she offered. "You have forgotten these visions. You must remember who you are, although you are afraid because you were killed for it in so many lives."

"I don't know what you mean," I replied.

"You have carried many powerful gifts through each life time. You were a great sorcerer. Powerful. You could levitate, disappear and reappear in another spot. You had the powers of a shaman, so powerful you could turn into an eagle and fly away. You evoked much fear in the hearts of men, even though you used your powers for good. You are afraid to remember because you were burned and killed in so many lives for these powers. In one life, when you were killed, they put ..." I cut her off and finished the sentence.

"They put a black shroud over me."

"Yes," she responded with delight that I could access that memory.

"I remember. As you started to tell me, I saw them draping the shroud on my body." Chills covered my body.

"You have many sorcerer guides, Merlin is one."

"I thought Merlin was a character in fiction."

"The character is modeled after the historical Merlin, a seer, who was adept in astrology, prophecy, and natural magic." She continued to work. "Now Kathy, if you concentrate, you'll remember your powers and be able to use them."

"I have never told anyone, but as a child I tried to move items with my mind. I concentrated with my eyes fixed on an object, as I tried with all my might to move it across the room. I was surprised and angry when it didn't move. I always thought objects could be moved with energy."

"You were able to do it, but let's focus on what's important right now - getting rid of pain from past lifetimes. Presently, you have taken on the heartache of your mother as your daughter has taken on yours." Her words sank into my chest like a sharp knife. I began to sob.

"Let go of it. You don't need to carry the pain and sorrow anymore. Take the shroud off."

My chest felt like it would burst. Her words made me cry harder.

"It's okay to cry. Just allow it. Let the pain go." Wiping the tears from my face, I let out a deep sigh. "I didn't realize how much emotional pain the body somatizes from this life as well as past lives."

She put her hand on my shoulder. "You did well – a lot of deep emotional release. From what I can see, you need to be working in the healing field." she said softly. "Helping people is your calling. Embrace it."

Millie was echoing what Marilyn had told me. These experiences further ignited my thirst for knowledge in the metaphysical world.

Part III – Association for Research and Enlightenment

Chapter 16

Finding my Mission in Life

I threw on my sneakers at 5 a.m. to stroll on the beach and meditate to sunrise. The view of the sky was breathtaking with shades of white, pink and orange blossoming over the horizon. A feeling of peace and serenity washed over me. I was ready to meet my group for breakfast.

This was my first trip to the ARE (Association for Research and Enlightenment) located on Virginia Beach in May 1995 for a conference called *What's My Mission in Life?* The institutes' teachings were based on the philosophy and methods of Edgar Cayce, an intuitive who gave over 14,000 readings until his death in 1945.

My friend Robert and I arrived in time for the Friday 7:00 p.m. "meet and greet." There were about a hundred people mulling around drinking refreshments, eating hors d'oeuvres and getting acquainted. After a while, the moderator asked us to form groups of seven. "For the next six days you are going to spend most of your waking hours with your group. Pick up a schedule before you leave. Every day we will meet from 8 a.m. until 9:30 p.m., with meal breaks and a half hour meditation. Have a nice evening and we'll see you in the morning."

Over breakfast my group had the opportunity to get to know one another. My group had people from different walks of life. Ricky owned a carpet cleaning business in New York. "My father, Fred, was a psychic medium. He held séances in the 1940s, long before they became popular. When we were kids, I remember him locating misplaced items in the house and he was able to read a person by holding a piece of their jewelry. I would love to do those things, but don't think I have that ability, so I'm here to learn more about my mission in life."

Lance who was in real estate shares the gift of telepathy with his sister. "Throughout our lives, I have communicated with her no matter how far apart we were. It taught me a valuable spiritual truth."

"What was that?" I asked.

"We are all connected. There is much more going on than we know. We have just begun to scratch the surface of what we can do with our minds."

Jonathan was an ex-partner in a multi-million-dollar business. "I got rich by living the universal law of abundance. I didn't even know it was a law. I just believed with every cell of my body and mind in abundance. I believed whatever I wanted would come to me and it did."

"Amazing. I wish I could do that," I said.

"You just have to believe it, feel it with every fiber of your being, and you will have it. The universe does not fail you when you know that abundance is there. I haven't worked for a year, but I'm not worried about making money." He shrugged his shoulders. "This year off was a blessing in disguise. It put me on the path to self-discovery."

"I used to teach at a university in New York, but now I have a consulting business," Tina offered. "What's really amazing is that I have up to a dozen dreams a night. As soon as I wake up, I write them down and analyze them."

Lance laughed. "I'm lucky if I can remember one dream!"

"Me too!" Ricky chimed in.

"I also studied for years to become licensed to sail a ship," Tina continued. "After the test, I was asked to teach the course. Eventually, I married one of my students. We bought ten acres of land, cut down trees, cured them for a year, and piece by piece, built our own sailboat to sail the Atlantic. The boat was then used for tours." Tina turned to Angie. "What about you?"

"I'm a telephone operator from Texas," she replied in her melodious drawl. "I love angels and communicate with them all the time." Angie was tall, fair complexioned, with beautiful sky-blue eyes, a welcoming smile, flowing wavy blonde hair, and a gentle disposition.

Our group leader, Dana, was a dream therapist who wanted to help other people interpret and utilize their dreams. She also had a black belt in karate. Dana looked at me. "What about you Kath?"

"I work in administration for a college. It's okay, but my passion is facilitating the healing process in others either with hands-on healing or words of comfort." I looked around, no one laughed. "To be honest, I was afraid that some of you might think that was weird."

Dana smiled. "As the days progress you will find that there are many people from different walks of life who have experiences beyond the physical in one way or another. Cast your worries aside. Psychic abilities, and spirituality could be freely discussed without fear of criticism. Everyone is here to share and learn."

We studied Cayce's readings on finding your purpose as well as the roadblocks to achieving goals. We filled out the SDS (Self-Directed Search) Assessment Booklet, A Guide to Educational and Career Planning. It measured competencies, activities you like to do, interests in occupations and a self-comparison with other people on traits such as mechanical, scientific, artistic, teaching, sales and clerical abilities. My results showed that I should be a career counselor, a secondary or pre-school teacher, or a teacher for gifted children. Not surprising, because I love to teach.

We worked on envisioning our ideals and how to use dreams as guidance. We discussed how to remember dreams, as well as different dream interpretation methods, such as finding the thematic pattern to a situation in your life and ways to move forward. The message in dreams could be bold and blatant or symbolic.

The next morning, Lance hobbled over to breakfast with a cane, pain blanketing his face. Sitting next to me, he grabbed my hand, put it on his knee and said, half serious, half laughing, "Use those healing hands on me."

I smiled and put one hand under and the other over his knee and began to channel energy.

He looked perplexed as he tilted his head. "I feel intense heat radiating into my knee. I can't believe it - feels a little better."

"That's great." I looked at my watch. "Time to go to the conference. I wish we had more time."

"Can you work on me tonight at my house?"

I nodded.

"I want to do something for you too. I don't live far from here so why don't you stay at my house for the rest of the week instead of a hotel? It will save you money. I have plenty of room, five bedrooms overlooking the water. In fact, you could stay longer if you like. What do you think?"

"Well, that's nice of you, but I'm here with my friend. Robert."

"Your friend is welcome too."

"Thanks for the offer, but I think we'll stay at the hotel. I still want to come over to work on you." At that moment, Robert came walking toward us. I introduced them, and they hit it off immediately, joking and laughing.

After dinner, we drove to Lance's house and parked in the driveway. The house was adjacent to an inlet. An expansive swimming pool with a Tiki bar adorned the yard. Looking up I saw a multi-level deck leading to a sunroom at the very top.

Lance greeted us at the door and I saw he winced in pain.

Since he was too uncomfortable to lie down, I motioned for him to sit in a chair by the window. I began working through his head chakra, about three inches above the fontanel point on the top of his head and moving energy down to the rest of his body. He felt it immediately.

"Your energy feels wonderful," he cooed.

I channeled the energy for about thirty minutes. Afterwards, Robert looked at me strangely and asked, "Were you putting energy in through his head?"

"Yes. Why?"

"Because **I saw it**," he whispered with surprise.

"What do you mean you saw it?"

"It was like a white beam of light coming out of your hands and going in through the top of his head. Then the two of you had a glow around you." His face turned more serious. "You know Kathy, I always believed you could do these things, but I never actually witnessed it with my own eyes. I blinked a few times to see if it was my eyes. Or maybe there was a light beaming from somewhere. But there wasn't. I can't explain it, but it was amazing."

I was taken aback at what Robert saw. I know that energy was coming out of my hands, because I felt it, but no one ever saw it. This was a physical confirmation that the transmission of energy was really happening.

Lance came over and put his hand on my shoulder. "Kath, I feel wonderfully relaxed."

"Glad to hear it. The energy will work over the next few hours, continue to loosen those tight muscles. Robert and I better get back to the hotel. We all have to be up early tomorrow."

Robert insisted we play the lottery on the way back to the hotel. He made me pick the numbers for four games. We found out my gifts lie in healing, not gambling.

The following morning, Lance showed up for group without a cane, walking straight as an arrow, no hint of pain in his face. Everyone commented on how well he looked and wanted to know what happened.

"Kathy came over last night and healed me," beamed Lance as he gave me a warm hug. "It was incredible. I can't thank her enough." He handed me two books, *Think and Grow Rich*, and *The Power of Positive Thinking*. "Kathy, I think you should read these books – they will help you envision and reach your goals. You can create whatever you want. I'm going to give you an affirmation. 'I am a spiritual being blessed with unlimited abundance.' I want you to say it frequently. Got it?'"

I nodded.

Originated during Edgar Cayce's lifetime, the Glad Helpers, meet in the meditation room of the ARE every Wednesday. They are a passionate group of people dedicated to helping individuals physically and mentally through meditation and prayer. Seating is set up with a few chairs in the middle for anyone who requests healing,

One day, instead of going to lunch, I decided to attend the meditation. As soon as I opened the door, I felt a *whoosh* of energy, yet I looked around and there was no fan or window open. The meditation had already begun, so I quietly took a seat in the back of the room. The room was plain and unadorned, clean and neat, filled with chairs facing the windows. I closed my eyes and began meditating. My throat and heart chakras started vibrating, very similar to when I was with Perry.

After a few minutes, I felt a dull pain in the middle of my chest. As I kept my attention on it, I had the sensation something was slipping out. In my mind's eye, I saw something leave my body, followed by a feeling of lightness. This "energy" went out the top of the building and flew around the area. Even though my eyes were with my body, I could still "see" everything as I went higher. My vision of the Earth was the same as if I were flying among the clouds. The houses and trees became little dots. Soaring higher and higher, I could no longer see detail. I was beyond the earth's atmosphere. The color indigo surrounded me. I felt as though I was covered in a tender blanket of peace and tranquility. While I was bathing in this euphoria, a loud noise in the meditation room startled me. My body jolted. In a flash, my energy and consciousness rushed back into my body. My eyes sprung open. I looked around. I was back in the meditation room. Not until I started walking back to the conference building, did I realize what had just occurred

– an out of body experience. (OBE)

Throughout the conference, we studied Cayce readings and how we could apply them to our lives. Cayce was a proponent of the Golden Rule, do unto others as you would have them do unto you. He also believed in karma, where everything you do has an end result that is either positive or negative. Born in 1877, his teachings were ahead of his time.

Each one of us was asked to keep a pen and paper by our beds and write down our dreams immediately upon awakening, while they were still easy to recall. The dreams were then studied in our group. There were other exercises such as shaping a mission statement, envisioning an ideal and studying our assets and strengths.

After just six days, our group had become closer than many people who know each other for a lifetime. We had laughed, cried and shared our innermost thoughts. I was free to be me and talk about my metaphysical experiences without judgement. It was comforting to know there were many other people sharing my thirst for knowledge in the metaphysical realm.

Chapter 17

We Don't Die

I loved my first trip to the ARE so much that six months later, I scheduled another for the conference, *We Don't Die.*

Rob Grant, author of the book, *Love & Roses for David*, was the first speaker. He explained how a near death experience (NDE) induced by LSD had changed his life. He said that LSD goes to the brain and endocrine system, causing hallucinations, and possibly blowing the Spirit (soul) out of the body. Essentially, it was a forced OBE.

He talked about how we are all part of God and death is a continuous experience for bringing us to a Divine state. We are here to learn lessons. Life's purpose is to help us reach a higher level of consciousness.

According to Grant, every time you meditate or do spiritual work, you raise souls along with your own. In essence you help them awaken to a higher level of consciousness.

Grant explained when a person is dying it is possible to see the soul going in and out of the body. (The conscious and unconscious) If a person dies suddenly such as in a car accident, they go through a "care center" to help with the transition because it takes time to shed the personality.

Rob's words triggered a myriad of thoughts and feelings. *It all fits. We are not separate from God, we just think we are. Life after life we keep coming back to grow spiritually.*

Being around the ocean feeds my soul so I find myself drawn to the beach at every opportunity. That first morning, at 5:30, I reached for my sneakers and walked to the beach. While most people were quietly tucked in their beds, I was blessed watching a magnificent sunrise.

The entire horizon had a layer of fiery red light glistening on the water. I felt the brisk salty air entering my lungs. It was cool and invigorating. I zipped up my sweatshirt as I watched and listened to the roar of the ocean. Pelicans and sea gulls flew and scanned the water for food, while tiny pipers, birds with pencil-point thin beaks, poked through the sand looking for food. About fifty pipers were moving in a sweeping motion back and forth, as the waves broke on the shore and retreated. They rushed in to poke at the wet sand hunting and eating tiny sea life. Then, in small groups of five or six they took baths, all huddled together. I was watching my very own nature show.

The horizon turned to orange, edged with a yellow hue, as the sun got ready to welcome the day. I caught the smell of a wood burning stove from where houses dotted the beach. I was completely immersed in the moment, drinking it in with feelings of joy and gratitude.

Back at the conference, the morning speaker was Dannion Brinkley, author of *Saved by The Light*, and *At Peace with The Light*. He emanated an exuberant energy delivered through his southern drawl. "Folks, I had a near death experience when I was on the telephone during a rainstorm and 180,000 volts of electricity shot through the telephone and killed me. I lay dead for 28 minutes. I saw and heard everything that was going on from a corner of the room, way above where my body lay stretched out on the floor. I saw my wife screaming and crying when she found my body and watched the medic trying to revive me."

"The saddest day of my life," said Brinkley, "was when the beings of light who approached me when I died, told me I was going back to my body." Before his NDE, Dannion said he was an angry, violent man who used his fists to solve problems. But when he came back, all that changed.

He looked around the room. "A piece of advice I have for all of you. "Forgive yourself and see the magnificence in yourself. By forgiving yourself, you can forgive others. Remember who you are, wonderful beings of light."

Besides his magnanimous personality, Dannion had a good sense of humor. "I know all of you came here to hear about dying. Well, this is going to be a short lecture because, guess what kids?" He looked around at each of one of us with a twinkle in his eyes. "There isn't any death! Sorry to disappoint you!" The audience resounded with laughter. "When people ask me if there is a hell, I say, I didn't ask, they, the beings of light, didn't bring it up."

His life changed dramatically after his NDE. Brinkley developed a great desire to help people and became a hospice volunteer, working with hundreds of people; some of them died in his arms. He said, "If you're there for someone going through the transition to death, they will be there when you are going through yours. Folks, you are insuring you won't be alone when you die."

Saturday, George Anderson, medium and author of the book, *We Don't Die*, gave us insight regarding the "other side" before he began connecting to relatives of members of the audience who had passed on. "Death," he said, "is like going from one room to the next. People have reported being met on the other side by their relatives and pets. Whatever people need to feel comfortable on the other side is given to them, especially if they experience a sudden death, such as an accident. Sometimes, they are met by children. Whatever it takes for a smooth and non-threatening transition."

Anderson shared his thoughts on ghosts saying they were actually souls afraid to go into the light for fear of judgment. Fear is the worst feeling of all; every other negative feeling such as anxiety and worry stem from it. On the other hand, forgiveness and love are more powerful than hatred.

Next, he discussed the Life Review. "The purpose of the review is to help the person who has passed on with spiritual growth; it is not given as a punishment. Everyone judges themselves, feeling the joy and pain they brought to people and animals." He cautioned, "Be careful of being intolerant of things you don't understand, such as different lifestyles. Anyone could be in that position in another life."

Anderson continued. "Prayer is the highest form of energy." People on the other side need our prayers to accelerate their journey to the light. When prayers are offered for someone else, it is more powerful than praying for yourself, and will come back to you tenfold. Offering prayers up for your enemies is even more effective."

Anderson was ready to begin connecting with relatives who had passed on. "All the spirits are pushing to come through first. They are all trying to talk through me at the same time." He told them to wait, then turned to the audience.

"I know each one of you hopes to hear from a loved one, but there are about five hundred people here, and only four or five people will come through from the other side. Don't be disappointed if you don't hear from your relatives. The most urgent messages will come through."

Like everyone else, I was hoping to hear from my brother or mother on the other side, but I didn't have any unfinished business with them due to an abrupt death or argument. I was at peace with just being part of the audience.

One woman's daughter, who had passed on in a horrible car accident, came through. "She wants me to tell you not to worry, she is all right. She is with her grandparents and they are all doing well." The woman broke down and cried.

"I'll be right back," I whispered to my friend, Robert. "Ladies' Room."

Walking down the hall, I saw Dannion Brinkley sauntering towards me. Looking at my Elton John/Billy Joel concert tee shirt, he smiled, and gave a "thumbs up," then wrapped his arms around me with a warm and gentle bear hug. "Great concert."

"Yes, I love them both," I chirped. Without forethought I said, "Dannion, can I ask you something?"

He crossed his legs at the ankles, put his hand on his chin and leaned against the wall. "Shoot."

"I have a serious question. My daughter is mentally ill, and I'm having a hard time dealing with it. Could you help me understand, so that I can handle it better? Or, why it happened?" I took a deep breath. "I can't believe I'm asking you this, but I feel since you have been to the other side, perhaps you can shed some light on it." My heart was heavy with grief. "And she's my only child."

Dannion saw how distraught I was. "Look into my eyes and hear what I'm going to say. First of all, you are not responsible. Let that sink in." He reached over and gave me a long, soulful hug, as I cried in his arms. My heart felt as though it would break. Then he pointed to his chest and in a serious tone with just a touch of levity said, "I'm half Swami, so listen to me, Darlin'!"

My whimpering morphed into a burst of laughter.

"You see the reason why this all happened is because you did something to her in a previous life and you wanted to live your own life in this one, so she's trying to get even with you. Is it working?"

I nodded.

"Now don't misunderstand. You didn't do anything wrong. You are entitled to have your own life, but it seems that your daughter interpreted this in a negative way. You and she were always best friends through many lifetimes. You'll always be best friends. Like a Bonnie and Clyde. Or better yet, like the two women in the movie, Thelma and Louise." He motioned like he was driving a car. "I could just see the two of you speeding down the highway in a convertible, her stepping on the gas, yelling Yahooooo!" He paused a moment and turned serious again. "You need to get the feeling of control back. The best thing you could do for her is to let go of the hurt and the pain. Our energy not only affects us, but also the energy of everyone around us. Including her. Don't judge, just send her your love and forgiveness."

"I have to remind myself - Thank you." I gave him a quick peck on the cheek and hurried back to Anderson's lecture. I couldn't help but think that meeting with Dannion was no coincidence. His words gave me perseverance and hope as the conversation flashed through my mind. *No matter what happens, I know it's karmic. I'll keep sending her love and prayers.*

Entering the room, I heard Anderson ask if anyone was related to a man named Harry who passed on. My friend, Robert, stood up along with a few other people. Anderson looked at each of the people standing trying to discern who was related to the Harry he was connecting with. Anderson turned to my friend Robert and asked, "Was Harry your father?"

"Yes."

"Well then, this message is for you." He motioned for Robert to come closer. "Everyone else can sit down. The message is for this gentleman. Your father says your mother is here too. Is that so?"

Robert nodded.

"Your father says, 'I'm sorry I was so distant and aloof when I was there. I always loved you but had a strange way of showing it.'"

My friend stared blankly.

Anderson continued. "I see a pipe. An Indian peace pipe. Does that mean anything to you?"

Robert shook his head, "No connection."

"Were you on bad terms when he passed on?"

"No. We were just distant."

"Your father says, 'I'm talking more now than I ever have before. I have grown. I'm sorry for what happened; it's just the way it was.' That's all ... I'm losing him.'" Robert was the last person in the audience to hear from a relative. Anderson was tired. The session was over.

While we were eating dinner, my friend realized the reading had more significance than he had originally thought.

"You know Kathy, it took time for me to figure out what Anderson was referring to. The saying 'It's just the way it was,'

was an expression my father always used when he was alive.'"
He took another bite of his sandwich. "The peace pipe had
significance. When my parents were in Europe they bought me
a peace pipe as a souvenir. It's hanging in my living room."

"Holy cow! He was right on target!"

"Kath, I don't know how it's possible, but I guess I did hear
from my father."

On the last day of the conference all the speakers sat on the
stage and the floor was opened to questions. I found one answer
particularly profound. A woman had asked, "How could my
daughter's suicide help my spiritual growth?"

Anderson paused a moment before answering. "Prior to this
happening, were you involved in the awakening of your soul?"

She thought for a moment. "No."

"Without her death, would you have been here?"

"I never would have ever given thought to any of this."

"Well, therein lies your answer."

His response resounded in my head. *Oh my God. I could
totally relate to this. My daughter's illness was the catalyst for
the road I'm travelling. Without her illness I would have been
happy to just live each day like a rat on a wheel, going through
the same motions. Never delving into the rich layers beyond
the physical. All the while I was looking for a sign, a teacher,
to lead the way, I realized that teacher was right in front of
me: my daughter. She taught me so many things including*

patience and unconditional love. I honor all that she is, and all
that she is not.

Robert and I left Virginia Beach refreshed and renewed. Learning that death is a transition to another plane is comforting. I felt like I was wrapped in a warmed baby bunting blanket. Driving home, we amused ourselves singing songs when suddenly the car started making loud popping sounds. Robert pulled over on a narrow shoulder. It was 7:30 and getting dark when we crossed into Maryland. A dusting of snow blanketed the grass.

"What do we do now Rob?"

"Don't worry. Someone will stop to help." We didn't have a cell phone, so we sat and waited. We flagged someone down and asked them to call the police. An hour later, no police.

"Well, Kath, it's after nine, what do you say we try to make it off the exit and find a place to stay for the night? It's dangerous to be on a small shoulder in the dark."

"I guess it's better than freezing in the car."

Robert drove slowly, all the while the car making loud pinging noises. We pulled into a 7-Eleven store. "There's a 76 truck stop a quarter mile down the road," offered the store owner.

We clunked along and pulled up to the stop. It seemed desolate, but a light was on in the garage, so Robert went in. Two minutes later, the garage door opened and he walked over to the car. "There's a mechanic inside. He said he would take a look under the hood."

"That's unbelievable. A mechanic at 9:30 on a Sunday evening?"

"I'll drive the car inside the garage, Kath. Why don't you come in and warm up?"

The mechanic was a man about sixty, with a weathered face, light sandy brown hair and a southern drawl. He looked at me with his crystal blue eyes and tipped his head. "Evening Ma'am. You look like you can use some hot coffee." He pointed to the coffee machine. "Go on - help yourself."

Within a few minutes he had inspected the car and gave us the verdict. "Well, I found the problem. A loose spark plug. I tightened it and you're good to go." He shut the hood with a loud bang.

"How much do we owe you?" Robert asked reaching in his pocket.

"Nothing," the mechanic answered. We insisted he take something for his time, but he held up his hand and shook it back and forth. "Not necessary. Just get home safe."

When we got in the car I looked at Robert. "We get stuck on a Sunday evening, find a truck stop with one man working by himself who fixes our car at no charge. What are the chances of that happening?" I took a sip of my hot coffee. "I think we just met an angel."

Part IV: Bridging Two Worlds Through Hypnosis

Chapter 18:

Up until now, my knowledge of hypnosis was limited and colored by the fictional character Svengali, an evil-looking musician and hypnotist who seduced, controlled, and exploited a young girl, molding her into a famous singer. The only other exposure I had was watching a hypnosis stage show where people did various inane and funny things, such as clucking like chickens.

After experiencing Kundalini energy, ETs, The Shekinah Fire, telepathy and various other forms of energy, I was ready to participate as an audience member observing a hypnosis demonstration. Little did I know how it would affect me.

Candy

"Can I have a volunteer?" asked Jack, a hypnotist at a weekend conference. "Who would like to experience remembering a past life?"

When Candy, a friend of mine, raised her hand, he motioned for her to sit in front of him in the center of the room. Once in trance, her body slumped over, Jack caught her before she could fall off the chair and gently propped her up. "Go through the "mist" to a lifetime that held significance for you and let me know when you are there." A few minutes passed; he repeated his request, but there was no response.

She looks lifeless. Has she passed out? Died? I've got to do something! Instinctively, I closed my eyes to find her. In a flash, I saw myself next to a child on a damp, dusty, dirt floor. People were hovering over us. *What's going on?*

The sound of Candy beginning to speak startled me. "I see horses ... and people walking in the street."

"Who are you?" the hypnotist asks.

"A mother." She starts to sob.

"Why do you cry?"

"Because I'm so poor ... My children are starving. I've just stolen food to bring back to them. We sleep on the dirt floor in the back of the blacksmith's barn." She begins to cry uncontrollably. Moments later she gained her composure. "The blacksmith ... feels sorry for me, so he lets us stay.

"Why are you there?"

"My husband died ... I have nothing."

Tears were rolling down my face. I *saw* what she was talking about. She had narrated the scene I was looking at. The blacksmith's sign. The mother's face painted with despair. Her long-tattered dress on a frail frame. Her eyes, portraits of sadness. Feeling the depth of her pain and helplessness, I forced my eyes open. *My God, the reason my vantage point was from the dirt floor was because I was one of her children!* **She was my mother.** This revelation kept me riveted while my head was spinning until Jack's voice grabbed my attention.

"Candy, now you can release your feelings of poverty and despair. They are no longer yours to keep. You are ready to experience abundance and hope." He paused a moment to allow his words to sink in. "When you open your eyes, you will feel refreshed and renewed."

Candy rubbed her eyes and looked around.

"How are you feeling Candy?"

"Okay, I guess."

Jack addressed the audience. "Through reincarnation, lessons are repeated until we learn what we need to learn. A guided past life regression helps to pinpoint where the life lesson originated and how to transcend the issue. As you have witnessed, Candy re-experienced a past life that left vestiges of thoughts and feelings that needed disclosure."

That afternoon, Candy's husband confessed that no matter how much money they made, she feared they would go broke. He didn't know why she worried so much since they had no money problems. Then it dawned on me; just as her fear of poverty stemmed from that life, so did mine. Candy's past life regression was just as much for me as it was for her. The universe has a way of orchestrating circumstances to help us, if we allow it. Over the next few months, I noticed my fear of poverty lessened, as did Candy's.

It's amazing how circumstances bring people together for their growth and development. Candy and I had been business acquaintances only a few months earlier, yet she was persistent in stopping by my office to say hello and calling me for lunch. In retrospect, I realize the mother-daughter bond from the previous life kept Candy coming back to start a friendship in this life and take care of unfinished business.

Chapter 19

Dungeon of Despair

Candy's past life regression piqued my interest to learn more about my other past lives. An opportunity arose to attend a group past life regression at a friend's house. Nothing had prepared me for what I was about to experience.

"Any part of your body that has tension or pain may have a physical manifestation from a previous life, where you were beaten, shot, burned, etc.," explained the hypnotist, Andy. "It can affect your life until you go back to that life and put the pieces of the puzzle together. When you feel the sensation and own it, you become free of it in this life. Emotions may have their roots in the past also." Andy gave each one of us a pencil and piece of paper with an outline of a body. "Draw lines on the parts of the body where you have pain. If you don't have any pain, then draw lines where you had surgery or even on a scar. If you are lucky enough to be free of physical issues, you can draw lines where you feel anxiety or fear."

I drew lines on the back of the neck and muscles on the jaw. Andy proceeded to put us in a meditative state and asked us to focus on the area we marked on our sheets.

As soon as I brought my focus to my neck and jaw, my consciousness flipped directly to feeling someone choking me. It felt real. My breathing was constricted. His thumbs were pressing hard right against my windpipe. *Dungeon ... I'm in a dungeon ...* Darkness and fear ... *I'm struggling to get free from this man, but I can't. I feel powerless.* I wrapped my fingers around his trying to pry them loose. *He's too strong.*

We were both men, clad in dirty clothes. The filthy stench of sweat filled my nostrils. I was rolling around getting beaten up and choked. I felt a pain in the back of my head as the other man hit my head on a stone sticking out of the dirt floor ... pain bolting through my head ... *Ugh* ... I felt blood trickle down the right side of my face. *I'm helpless ... Can't shake his hold loose. My arms are getting tired from the struggle ... no way out.* I was giving up ... letting go ... life leaving my body.

Then I heard Andy's voice telling us to come back. I felt myself slowly coming back into the room. I was there, but part of me was still on the floor, experiencing death. I felt frightened and sad. Unfortunately, Andy was unable to work with us individually, and the pain and trauma associated with the event was still haunting me. I desperately needed closure.

When I got home, I went into meditation and led myself back to that life. I relived the scene and allowed myself to be present with the feelings. While entranced, I learned a powerful lesson. The exact words I used in that life, "I am powerless. I am helpless," were words carried over to this life.

They hung over me like a dark cloud. To counteract the cloak of malaise I created a positive affirmation: "I am powerful. I have choices. I am surrounded by a golden healing light."

Between the regression, and affirmations, I was able to release the pain and get closure. I needed to experience that horrible death and harrowing feelings. The more I owned it, the freer I became. Energy shifted. It was shocking to see how subconscious memories from past lives can hinder our present lives and when exposed, astounding how they can help heal patterns of pain and trauma.

After that experience, I could see how hypnosis could be a great healing modality. It led me to read the book *Many Lives, Many Masters*, by Dr. Brian Weiss, a traditional, psychiatrist. In 1980 when a patient came to him with anxiety and panic attacks, his skepticism about reincarnation was challenged. While in hypnosis, she went back to over 80 past lives and was able to recall names, how she died and what her karmic lesson was. Ultimately, she became completely well. At one point, she channeled messages about the doctor's son who had passed away. He is well known for his work with past lives therapy. After reading that book, I went for hypnosis training.

Chapter 20

John

"Over thirty years have passed, and we've run into each other," John raved over lunch. "I mean, what are the odds? We have a lot of catching up to do."

"Since the last time we spoke, a lifetime ago in Brooklyn, things have changed significantly. Besides being divorced and navigating the challenges of having a mentally challenged daughter, I'm an intuitive, a hypnotist, and energy healer."

He frowned. "I'm sorry to hear about your daughter, that must be a monumental challenge." John sipped his hazelnut coffee. "You're kidding about hypnotizing and healing people, right?"

I shook my head.

"Can you hypnotize people to find out if they lived before?"

Although he didn't believe he could be regressed to a past life, he was fascinated with the topic. I offered to work with him in exchange for repairs I needed around the house.

In the first session, I took him back through the years in his present life. He told me of a disturbing event that happened when he was a teenager, something no one outside his family was aware of. When out of trance, he didn't think he told me anything since he didn't remember anything. When I relayed the story he told me, he was shocked he revealed something buried so deep.

"I'll tape the next session, so you can hear for yourself."

The following week, once in hypnosis, I suggested he go back to a previous life which held great significance for him. He went back to a life as a Native American named Sagawan who lived in the woods with a woman, Naga.

"What are you wearing?"

"Boots and leggings ... made of hide."

"Can you describe Naga to me?"

His face developed a warm smile. "Naga has long black hair ... I love her very much ... We are happy."

"Are you married?"

His smile disappeared; his face turned ashen. "No. We live together with child."

He seemed disturbed to be unmarried. "Let's move forward to when you pass on in that life." He started clutching his chest. "What's going on?"

"Pain in my chest ... hard to breathe."

Jesus, he's reliving a heart attack! I must think quickly. "Okay, John, step out of the body, and watch what's going on as a bystander. You will no longer feel pain; you will just see what is going on as though you are watching a movie." His breathing slowed; the tension was released from his face.

"No more pain ...Very serene ..." He had passed on in that life. I brought him back into the room and played back the tape. He was speechless.

The following week, I taped another session. He went under much more quickly this time.

"Many people running after me."

"Why?"

"They want to hurt me. They think I'm crazy because I say I can see the future. I'm running fast ... They still chase me ... They call me a witch ... They are English, not from England though ... from the new land."

"Where is that?"

"Salem."

"What is your name?"

"Paul."

"How do you tell the future?"

"I see things ... feel things."

"Do you use any instruments?"

"Pentagram. I use the five points, the moon, sun and planets." He gets distracted. "They are banging on my house ... Jenny, my wife is dead." He clenches his fist. "Bitch ... I hate her. Bitch!"

"Is this woman someone you can identify in your present incarnation?" Without hesitation he named his ex-wife. "How did she die?"

"Killed her ... My hands ... choked her. Whore ... tormented me. I had to run to the country where it's peaceful ... Met Naga in the woods ... Lived together. Much love between us." His face changed from total disgust to peace.

"Didn't you say your name was Paul?"

"Yes, it was, but Naga gave me an Indian name, Sagawan. It meant "lonely one.""

"Why didn't you marry Naga?"

"No one in the woods to marry us ... alone with our child."

"I see. Now put your index finger and thumb together to "anchor" the happy feeling you had with Naga. You can choose to feel that happiness anytime when you need to by putting your thumb and pointer fingers together. We are going to leave this life now bringing all the good feelings and going to another life which held significance for you."

John went back to a life as a Buddhist monk in a temple in the Himalayan Mountains. He described what he saw. "Many candles ... smell incense burning ... much praying." His hands rose about six inches from where they rested on his thighs. Slowly, he turned them palm up and started to chant "om." I stared at him, mouth agape. *John has never meditated and here he is chanting!* When he stopped, his hands began moving slowly in the air, as if he were feeling or sensing with his fingers. Fascinated, I watched until he began to speak.

"I see ... I feel ... many souls changing faces ... always the same souls ... I feel the light of God shining down, filling the soul ... all powerful, all loving ... Peace ... Joy ...The road to happiness is the road from the past ... The road to the highest is the road from the lowest ... To see is to be born blind ...To be born blind is to see."

I watched him closely as he fell silent. "John, what's happening now?"

"I see a Rabbi." His eyes were moving under his lids as though he was concentrating, listening before he spoke again. "The road through life is one of loneliness. The journey starts in the hereafter and ends when we are born ... The track is straight, the road is narrow ... Peace is from within ... Peace is not found, it is earned ... The journey never ends ... star to star ... heaven to heaven ... light to light. The light is one ... pure ... the light is all. Symbols ... arrows, dots, notes equal God ... Aleichem, malachim." He continued inaudibly for a few minutes then segued into a chant ... "ommmmm."

"John! John!" I called trying to get his attention. He was still chanting. I called louder. "John, look in a book and tell me the date."

With eyes closed his nose and forehead wrinkled. "Scrolls. There are no books ... Scrolls. "Observing this lifetime, what did you learn?"

"Love, kindness, teach others, peace, tranquility ... The soul seeks peace in the universal soul ... The soul is the center of the universe...Conquer evil with white light."

"Beautiful! Now let's move to the end of that life; tell me what you see."

"Die ... Very old ... alone ... pain ... Soul flying away in peace." He let out a sigh of relief.

"Okay, now you are going to come back to your present incarnation. I will count from one to ten. At ten you will be fully awake in your present life."

He wasn't back. He didn't move. "John, where are you?"

There was a long pause. "Don't want to come back," he whispered.

He can't do this! This is not supposed to happen! I was shocked at his refusal. "You must come back. On the count of three you will return into the room."

"No ... Stay here ... in the light ... God's light."

He had an enviable peaceful look on his face. *Shit! I must get him to come back.*

"You must return to your present incarnation," I commanded. "There are reasons why you are here, things you must experience before you leave. Family and friends. But, I will tell you this. You can bring the white light that you feel now back with you. You can feel that sense of calm and tranquility. I will give you a few minutes to feel it and take it with you." I waited. "It is time now. You can begin to return. I'm going to count from one to five. At five you will be fully awake. One ... two ... three ... starting to come back into the room ... four, bringing back what you need ... five, fully awake and present in this room."

His eyes opened. He looked half asleep. "Did anything happen?"

"Yes. You went in deep again. Were you totally unaware of where you went?"

He nodded.

John listened to the recording, hearing for the first time what transpired. He was astounded. Even though he heard his voice on tape, he said, "I can't believe that was me. I sounded so philosophical!" His eyes widened. "Some of it sounded like a foreign language."

"John, you spoke so eloquently. Your words were spiritually illuminating. I've never heard you talk like that before!"

"I'm as amazed as you are!" He looked down at his hands. "I'm shaking! I don't even know what I was talking about. Do you?"

"I think so." I looked down at my scribbled notes for a few minutes. "You said, 'Many souls that change coats, put on new faces, always the same souls.' The coats are physical form, the new faces are the personalities in each life, and the same souls tell us we don't shed our underlying essence. Then you said, 'we go from life to life,' which of course, is reincarnation. The journey that starts in the hereafter and ends when we are born. Although this is the period between our lives, it seems to be a time that is active and meaningful. Supposedly, we do a lot of work in that space between lives."

I referred to my notes. "The track is straight, the road is narrow," implies there is only one way, through the Divine. When you said, 'the journey never ends, star to star, heaven to heaven,' that too is referring to reincarnation. The light is one, means we are all one. Symbols, arrows, dots equal God. I think you were seeing the written Word in symbols or a different language. There was more, but it definitely wasn't in English."

"I can't believe it. Where did I get all that from?"

"John, I think you tapped into the universal consciousness. Your experience is having a powerful impact on my worldview."

"You and me both."

The following week I mentioned the occurrence to a friend. She said, "Write down the words phonetically, I know someone who may be able to translate it." Although I wanted to believe John spoke a foreign language, I was expecting gibberish. John hadn't taken any language courses; he did not go to college. He was 100% Italian, lived in Italy as a child and still lived in an Italian section of Brooklyn.

A week later I got a call. "Kathy, I have some exciting news for you. My friend translated those words." Her voice resounded in my brain.

"You are kidding, aren't you?"

"No. John spoke Hebrew."

"Holy cow! What did he say?"

"Alacheim is plural for upon you, or with you. Malach is one angel, so malachim is angels. Put it together and he said, "There are angels upon you." The other words were unidentifiable. He thought they were Persian or something."

I mulled over what just transpired. John spoke another language, and had delivered such a beautiful, loving message. I felt the impact. I felt surrounded by the presence of angels. I heard a voice in my head say, *"We've been here all along, right by your side. Sometimes you feel alone because you don't give us the chance to help you!"*

Everything that happened seemed surreal. Like a sci-fi movie. From accessing someone else's past life in real time, to hearing a dead language from someone else's regression. How much information is out there that we are unaware of? Are there dimensions that we have not accessed? Maybe it's a matter of tuning into the right frequency, like on a radio?

Chapter 21

Ellie

Ellie, a woman in her late twenties, was seeking answers to a challenge she was facing. With no close relatives, Ellie felt quite alone. Although she felt it wasn't possible to be regressed to a past life, she was open to possibility.

Once Ellie was in a deep relaxed state, I asked, "Go back in time where you first felt alone. Once you get there, let me know by nodding your head or lifting your thumb." After a few moments, she nodded her head.

"Good. Now look down at your feet. What do you see?"

"Old leather shoes."

"What are you wearing?"

"Cotton ... very coarse."

"Are you male or female?"

"Male ... about sixteen ... Long brown straight hair."

"Look around. Are you inside or outside?"

"Outside ... It's foggy."

"What year is it?"

"1589."

"Now look around for your home. When there, describe it for me."

She hesitated. "No house ... Bungalow .... I live with my grandma. Emily. Can't leave her, she has no one else. Must take care of her. I love her. She raised me. Very old. No teeth. Sits in a rocking chair, a scarf draped on her head."

"Very good. What else do you see?"

"The floor is covered with a red, brown, and green kilim." (a pileless tapestry, woven carpet, or spread made somewhere in the Middle East such as Turkey, Kurdistan, the Caucasus, Iran, or western Turkestan.) Ellie stopped speaking for a moment, although she seemed deep in thought.

"I have hunting material on the floor ... I hunt deer ... I am the man of the house. Must hunt and kill to eat."

"What did you learn in this life?"

"Responsibility ... Love."

"Okay. Let's leave that life. Back to the space between lives. Approach another life that has meaning for you. Let me know when you are there."

After a few moments, she nodded her head.

"Describe what you see."

"I'm wearing black shiny high heels, white stockings, and red lipstick ... I'm tall and thin ... Navy polka dot outfit and hat. My hair is short and blonde ... I'm smoking. Waiting impatiently on the street for my driver."

"Do you know what year it is?"

Without hesitation, she responded. "1923. Chicago."

"Do you know your name?"

"Ruth Watkins Wilson. That's my name."

"How old are you?"

"I'm in my mid-thirties. Maybe thirty-five ... Married to a wealthy man, Max ... He wears expensive suits and ties ... He's not honest."

"What does he do for a living?"

"Something to do with a bank, I'm not sure what though. That's where I met him ... I used to work there."

"Were you born in Chicago?"

"No. Max was ... My mom was from the Netherlands. But I feel I lived in the Northeast before I moved to Chicago."

"Are you happy?"

Her face turned sullen. "No. My father was an alcoholic. He beat my mother until one day she took me and my sister and left ... She worked as a secretary. I married Max because I wanted to have money, nice clothes ... security."

"Do you have children?"

"No. But I see a little boy ... I think he's my sister's child. He's very dear to me. I love him like my own." She let out a deep sigh. "I don't think I know how to find meaning in life. All I look forward to is throwing big parties."

She fell silent. I could see by the somber look on her face, she was processing information. A few moments later, she continued.

"Oh God. I have become rigid and resentful like my mother ... Not much of a relationship with her but my sister and I are close." She pauses.

After a few moments I prompted her to move on. "Let's go forward a few years. What is going on now?"

"I'm dressed in black. My eyes are swollen from crying ... Max died ... Heart condition. I am sad and happy."

"Why both feelings?"

"Max kept me in a style of living way above that of most other people. I had parties and lots of material things. Yet, I'm glad he's dead, because I don't have to live behind a facade any longer ... I'm free."

"Let's move forward to your passing in that life."

Ellie gathered her thoughts, "I'm in the hospital. Sixty-something years old ... asthma. My nephew is comforting me ... I'm leaving him all my money ... He will be able to go to college ... have a good life ... I'm at peace now." Her face relaxed.

"You can leave that life behind now." I waited a moment then asked, "What did you learn from this lifetime?"

"I was materialistic. Didn't know how to love ... used my husband to have a good life. But money and possessions didn't make me happy."

Ellie had been under for more than an hour. Time to bring her back.

"Before we come back, I want you to remember the deep love you felt for your sister and nephew and the lesson learned so that you can bring this knowledge back with you. You can carry that love in your heart forever. Take any other information which will help you in your present incarnation."

When Ellie came out, tears were running down her face. "I feel strange. Like I was really there."

I handed her a box of tissues. "Ellie, that's normal. Whether or not the PLR was real or imaginary it served a purpose. You experienced deep familial ties somewhere in the recesses of your mind. It shows that you are capable of feeling love."

Ellie's regression to the 1920's was so detailed, I searched the *New York Times* and *Chicago Tribune* on microfilm in the 1920's looking for Max and Ruth Wilson. I called the Chicago county clerk's office, but to no avail. Perhaps it was there, maybe in another town somewhere and I hadn't located it. Years later this past life regression still haunted me, so I decided to once again try my luck finding Max and Ruth Wilson through the Internet. On ancestry.com I found a Max Wilson born about 1895 and married to Ruth. They lived in Sioux City

Iowa. This was recorded in the Iowa State Census collection of 1836-1925. Sioux City is only 510 miles from Chicago. Could this be the Max and Ruth Wilson I was looking for? Could Max have relocated to Chicago when he got older? That remains a mystery.

Chapter 22

George

George and I had been friends for years before he asked me to help him with a lifelong issue. "I feel if I do something wrong, I'll be cut off from the world, alone and in complete darkness. I can't shake the feeling, and I want to find out where the fear originated. Another thing that plagues me," George recounted, "was when I was seven years old, my father had a heart attack on my birthday. I didn't want any other birthday parties after that because I didn't want to take any chances that somehow, I may have caused my father's heart attack. Maybe I could cause other bad things to happen."

"Over fifty years is a long time to be carrying that heavy load around."

"I've tried different things, but nothing has been able to help me shake the feeling."

I closed my eyes and connected with George's energy field, scanning his body in my mind's eye to find the age when these feelings materialized. I felt an "energy knot." A time frame gelled in my mind. "What occurred when you were around eight years old?"

"When my mother got angry with me, she wrapped me in a blanket and put me in the bathtub in the dark."

George's demeanor changed. "What did that little boy feel when he was in the bathtub?" I gently prodded.

"I was reaching out for comfort, but didn't get any," he said sadly. "I felt totally isolated and alone. Afraid to make a mistake or ask for anything. Afraid they would put me back in the darkness."

"Okay, it's good that you could connect with that feeling. Now, let's relax a little deeper. Let's go back to age seven, six, five, four, all the way back to three, all the way down to two, one and then back to when you were in utero." I observed George intently. "Now, go back to the time before you were born. That time between lives." He was quiet. "George, what's going on?"

Slowly, he responded. "I don't know who I am, but I am aware that I am. The only way to explain it is I am "just consciousness." He took a few minutes before he continued. "I feel like I am in touch with my mother's feelings about me, negative feelings. Always anticipating something bad was going to happen."

When it seemed that was all he could remember, I progressed him to his birth and asked, "What's going on now?"

"All this traumatic stuff all around ... lights ... people ... scary." He paused for a few minutes. "I'm tuning into my mother's feelings of sadness. Hmmm ... Feeling really bad ... No connection with the world. I realize that was the feeling I had before I was born."

"George, that's an excellent observation. Now let's work on releasing some of the feelings you are experiencing. Let me show you the Emotional Freedom Technique (EFT), which combines tapping on certain meridian points while saying a pertinent phrase. These are the same points used in acupuncture to release the electrical charge associated with an unpleasant feeling or memory. Would it be okay for me to tap on some points on your head, chest and arms?"

He nodded. I tapped on points while repeating his words out loud, "alone... cut off from the world ... darkness ... no comfort." I waited for him to process his feelings. "Now, imagine that you were welcomed into the world and loved. Imagine that your parents looked forward to your birth with anticipation and love." By the euphoric look on his face, he was totally immersed in these feelings. "Let's tap in those feelings now ... joy ... love ... connection."

When I guided him back to the present, he said he felt better, but he needed time to process the session.

A few days later, George called. "For the first time in my life, I don't feel if I do something wrong now I would be put back in that dark place. I don't feel anything is wrong with me anymore. A lot of anxiety has dissipated. Now I can have a negative thought and I'm able to let it go."

After releasing those negative beliefs at 60 years old, he entered a relationship with a woman and found genuine happiness.

"We get along really well," George said. "I can't imagine life without her."

Chapter 23

Barbara

Barbara, a woman in her mid-forties, arrived for a hypnosis session, chattering nervously, and fidgeting with her fingers.

"I'm shy and find it hard to start a conversation with people. I don't know if I'll say the right thing, you know? And I was nervous coming here because I don't think I can be hypnotized, and if I can be hypnotized, well, maybe I would lose control."

"You are not alone in your thinking. It is common for people to think that they cannot be hypnotized or afraid they would relinquish control to the hypnotist. The truth is, Barbara, almost anyone can be hypnotized. The key is allowing yourself to relax your conscious mind so that deeper levels can be accessed. Secondly, you will remain in control of yourself. Your resourceful mind would not let you do anything you would not feel safe doing. Besides, I wouldn't ask you to do anything crazy like bark like a dog, or cluck like a chicken"

She let out a strained laugh and took a deep breath.

I continued, speaking in a soft voice. "Some people find it helpful to imagine we are playing a game. They allow themselves to have fun with it. Could you give yourself permission to do this?"

She nodded.

"Great. Once you are in a deeply relaxed state, you may think what you see, or feel is not real, but say it aloud anyway. Remember, we're just having fun." Using visualization techniques, Barbara's face softened. Her eyes began to flutter, signaling deep relaxation.

"Find a feeling or event that would be helpful." A few minutes later, Barbara began to speak.

"I see an eagle flying in the sky ... it's coming towards me ... strange."

"What's going on?"

I'm becoming the eagle ... so high in the sky ... flying ... looking down at grass ... trees."

Her eyes were closed, but her head was moving as though scanning the landscape. Her face was glowing.

"What are you feeling right now?"

"Pride. The eagle is filled with pride."

"Anything else?"

"I can feel its strength ... and freedom." She was breathing slowly and rhythmically.

"Wonderful!" I envied her apparent euphoria. "Before we move on, bask in the feelings. When you are ready, let's go to another life."

After a few moments Barbara began speaking again.

"I see an Indian village ... by a river ... watching from above ... they are dressed in skins."

"Barbara, what else do you see?"

"The women are talking ... I can't understand what they are saying...different language. They are squatting washing clothes." She continued to observe. "I'm slowly moving closer to the people in the group ... they are smiling at me ... gesturing to come closer ... Hmm ... I feel like I am one of them ... no longer a bystander."

"Wonderful. Feel those loving feelings and allow them to penetrate every cell of your being. Then as we start to come back into the room, take those loving feelings with you."

She began to pout.

"Barbara, what's wrong?"

"Don't want to come back ... I feel so good."

"Those feelings are within you. You can take them with you wherever you go. They were always there, you just couldn't access them before. Do you know this to be true now?"

She took a moment. "Yes," she whispered.

"Good, let's start our journey back." When Barbara opened her eyes, she embraced me.

"I didn't know I could feel so much love!"

"You allowed yourself to feel what was already there. You just had to be in a space to access and identify those feelings. Barbara, you gave yourself a wonderful gift."

Although I cannot empirically prove one can experience a past life under hypnosis, I cannot explain how an Italian man can speak Hebrew or people can connect with loving feelings or even have emotional or physical healings. I do believe that we are more powerful than we think and our resourceful minds can bring up circumstances, real or imagined, that highlight issues for resolution. Past life regression, EFT and other modalities can have a real effect on how we think, act and impact others.

My experiences in this new world filled me with wonder and eager anticipation of each new day. However, nothing had prepared me for what ensued.

Chapter 24

Antonitus

The Song of the Thorn Bird
"According to legend, the thorn bird sings just once in its life. Leaving its nest, it searches for a bush with long, sharp thorns. Upon finding such a bush it impales itself on the biggest thorn. At that moment it begins to sing.
"The bird out-carols the lark and the nightingale and the world pauses to listen. God smiles with pleasure at the captivating melody. What is the message of this sacrificial music? Life's most satisfying moment can be purchased only at the price of great pain – so says the legend..."
Fr. Fernand Kathista, Author

If I had known on that balmy August evening what was eventually going to unfold, I would have never handed Michael my raffle ticket at the dance. What was it about him that drew me, so close that I couldn't see? Maybe my radar was disengaged by his irrefutable charm, and soft-spoken voice.

There was absolutely no hint of foreboding in my usually keen sense of intuition. Well, at least not at first, because emotional involvement seemed to foster rationalization, superseding pure logic.

It all started when Gina, a bubbly, sassy, and extremely

opinionated friend called this one Friday night.

"Kath, where do you want to go tonight?"

"It's been a long week. I just want to curl up in front of the TV with an ice cream sundae and zone out."

"You know when we go out, you always perk up and have a good time. C'mon, say yes."

I relented. "Okay, Okay."

"Great! Let's meet at The Inn at 10."

I arrived at the club and found Gina sitting at a table by the door. I gave her a hug and sat down. The music was contemporary rock, with some old favorites that always makes me feel like dancing and singing.

When the buffet table was set up, Gina and I quickly joined the line. The food at The Inn was delicious. On the menu was Penne alla Vodka, Chicken Francaise, as well as a salad with olives and feta cheese. Dessert consisted of brownies and chocolate chip cookies. After a cup of coffee and dessert, Gina and I got up to dance.

"Look at that guy on the left side of the bar," Gina said, leaning over to me. "He's really cute and he keeps staring over here. I think he's staring at you." I turned around and spotted him.

"Maybe he's looking at you."

"I don't think so girlfriend. Take another look, his eyes are following you around the dance floor."

"You've got some imagination, Gina!"

Right after the music stopped, I walked over to the bar to get a drink and glanced in his direction. He was even better looking up close. He was tall, olive-complexioned and handsome. His short dark wavy hair had patches of silver-grey on the side. He must have felt my gaze because he turned and looked me squarely in the eyes. I felt my face flush, so I quickly offered a polite smile and turned away.

As I got my drink, raffle ticket numbers were being called for the door prize. Everyone was checking their ticket stubs. I searched my bag for my ticket, while trying to remember the numbers by repeating them over and over. When I pulled out the stub, I realized I couldn't see the numbers. *Dammit, my reading glasses are home!* At that point, I turned to this man who was standing close by.

"Could I ask you to read my numbers? My glasses are home and these numbers are tiny!" I extended the ticket in my hand.

"Sure." He read them off. "No, these aren't the winning numbers. Sorry." Without hesitation he extended his hand and smiled. "By the way, my name is Michael."

As soon as our fingers touched, I felt a flash of electricity run through my body.

"Kathy. Thanks for reading my numbers."

"Anytime," he quickly replied. "Always willing to rescue a damsel in distress. Actually, it's what I do, well, sort of."

"Okay, I'll bite. What do you do, Michael?" I was intrigued.

"I'm a firefighter in Queens. I've had some close encounters with death and injuries to my neck and back." He pointed to his lower back and a scar on the right side of his neck. "Causes me some pain, but nothing I can't live with."

"Sounds like a dangerous job."

"Yea, but I love it. I get a lot of satisfaction when I rescue people. As an EMT, I give talks about safety, prevention of injury and what to do in an emergency. Enough about me, what do you do?"

"My job is not as exciting as yours. I sit at a desk, do paperwork and go to meetings. The benefits are great. Pays the bills." I almost mentioned my background as a hypnotist, and energy healer but thought better of it since it was non-conventional and misunderstood in the 90's.

It was easy talking with Michael. Looking into his almond brown eyes, he seemed to be carrying around an unshakeable sorrow which I wanted to reach out and heal. Although I wondered what it was, I kept my curiosity to myself. The conversation was kept light, centering on food, music and travel. Before we knew it, they were cleaning up tables, shutting off lights and closing the place down.

"I guess we have to leave before they throw us out," I said with a laugh.

"Can I walk you to your car?"

"Yes. I'd like that especially since the parking lot is dark and deserted."

Once we reached my car he said, "Nice talking to you," and walked to his truck. He didn't ask for my telephone number and I didn't offer. *That's strange. We seemed to have a connection.* I glanced at his truck as he drove away. *I wonder if I will see him again.*

Driving home, I realized I was so enamored with Michael, I hadn't said goodbye to Gina.

The following morning, I called to apologize.

"It's okay, Kath. Besides, you two seemed to really hit it off. I didn't want to interrupt you guys. So, when are you going to see him again?"

"That's just it. I thought we had a good time, but he never asked for my number."

"Maybe he was just looking to talk with someone." A moment later, Gina let out a howl. "Oh my God, I bet he's married!"

"I guess that could be a possibility." I felt a gnawing pain in the pit of my stomach.

I couldn't get this man out of my mind. Was the attraction real or imagined? I went over the conversation with Michael in my head, his smile and body language.

A few weeks later, Gina, and I went to Quincy's, a nightclub in Teaneck, New Jersey. Being preoccupied with looking around the room searching for Michael, I wasn't having a good time. I picked up my pocketbook and jacket.

"You're leaving already?" Gina said brusquely, looking at her watch. "It's early!" "Yes, I'm feeling bummed."

"When are you going to stop brooding over that guy? Time to move on, Kath!"

"You're probably right. Talk to you tomorrow." I gave Gina a hug and left.

I was obsessed with finding Michael. I couldn't tell Gina I was going to make a last-ditch attempt tonight by stopping by the Inn. I promised myself that if he wasn't there, I would forget about him.

The place was packed. Squeezing my way through the crowd to some friends, I tried to look interested in their conversation but was preoccupied searching for Michael. Then my gaze settled on one table. There he was across the room, with a woman. I could feel my face flush. I turned away and started walking to the Ladies' Room. Fumbling for a mint in my purse, I glanced up and found Michael directly in my path. He was smiling, waiting for my eyes to catch his gaze.

"Hi. How are you?" he beamed. He seemed happy to see me.

"Good," I said coolly, while my claws began to emerge. "Is your girlfriend okay with you coming over to me?"

"She's not my girlfriend. She's just someone I know. "Look, I'm going to be honest with you; I've been looking for you for the past few weeks. I've been going crazy running around to every club hoping to run into you again."

I felt my body tingle. "You have?" I had to contain my excitement.

"Yeah. I thought I would bump into you somewhere." His face turned serious. "You know, when I walked you out to your car the night we met, I realized I said goodnight and walked away, and didn't even ask if you wanted to meet again for coffee or lunch or something. That was really lame. Anyway, I haven't stopped looking everywhere." A warm smile blanketed his face. "I'm really glad to see you."

I couldn't believe his candor. "Yeah, me too."

The DJ was playing the song, One More Night, by Phil Collins. Michael reached for my hand and ushered me to the dance floor. When he gently put his arm around my waist and pulled me in a little closer, I felt a rush of excitement travel up my spine.

Before I left, this time we exchanged telephone numbers and made plans to meet the following weekend.

The Bodyguard with Kevin Costner and Whitney Houston was the movie of choice for our first official date. Michael clutched a large bucket of popcorn drowned in butter, while I opted for my favorite - Raisenets.

After the movie, we went to a diner. Michael wanted a cup of black coffee.

"None for me. It'll keep me up all night. But I could go for a peppermint tea." As we were talking, the voice in my head was echoing a name. "Who's Kitty?"

He shot me a glaring glance. "How did you come up with that name?" Wonder blanketing his face.

"Why? Does it mean something to you?"

"Well, yes. My daughter's name is Karen. Kitty is her nickname." He stared at me. "You're freakin' me out." I know I didn't mention her name."

"No but I get feelings and impressions. Names in peoples' energy fields pop up. Is she okay?"

"Yeah, it's just that my ex, Viola, has been giving me a hard time about seeing her. Vy is just a bitch and she's done whatever she could to make me miserable. I really miss Kitty." He quickly changed the subject. "So, what do you want to do on our next official date?" He managed a faint smile.

The following Saturday, we went on a hike in Harriman Park. After an hour, we stopped by a lake. There was no wind. The water was glimmering like a sheet of glass. You could see the brilliant reflection of trees in the water. As I looked out at the panoramic view, I felt his gaze on my face and turned toward him.

He smiled as he outlined my face with a gentle touch of a finger. "I really like your profile– the soft lines around your eyes and chin, your nose. Do you have Native American blood in your ancestry?"

"Not that I know of. But there was a medicine man named White Eagle who is my Reiki Guide in this life. We were together in a past life where he gave me the name, White Rain, which means snow."

"You lost me!"

"Okay, let me back up. I have a practice in the healing arts." I waited for a reaction, maybe a cynical retort; but there was none. "I was trained in Reiki, a Japanese hands-on healing system. The practitioner channels energy through her hands into a person to activate their natural healing abilities. When I went for the training, I asked my higher self who my Reiki Guide was. I saw in my mind's eye a weathered, old, Indian dressed in his traditional regalia, with a magnificent feathered headpiece. He told me his name was White Eagle. When I channel healing energy during a session, I call him in to help along with other guides and entities."

Michael was listening intently. "How'd you get these abilities?"

"First of all, everyone has intuitive abilities, but some people may never access them. Some sense things in times of a loved one's death or other events in their lives. Oftentimes, they chalk it up to coincidence or some other random occurrence. In truth, they accessed a group consciousness. When people tap into this ability, more intuitive energy flows. It's like tuning into a radio frequency. Anyone can do it, including you."

He chuckled.

The next few months were lighthearted and enchanting. Michael kept his mountain bike at my place. On weekends, we played paddleball and traversed mountain paths in the Hudson Valley. Rainy days, we watched movies and played cards. He was crazy about a card game I taught him from my childhood, Russian Solitaire.

Michael was soft spoken and a good listener. When I was tense, his voice calmed me. There was never a hint of annoyance or frustration in his tone of voice or body language.

One day, as we were sitting in an ice cream shop, I started talking about past life regressions and how revisiting a past life could help resolve issues in a present life.

Without hesitation, Michael asked, "Could you regress me?"

"Sure. I would be happy to."

Michael slapped his knee with his hand. "Great. Then let's do it."

The following weekend we had an elaborate barbecue. After dinner, he said he was ready.

I ushered him over to the recliner chair. "Michael, get comfortable. Take your shoes off if you'd like. I'm going to use a progressive relaxation technique to help calm your conscious mind so that your subconscious can be accessed."

Once he was in trance, I asked, "Michael, go back to a lifetime which held significance for you. It could be one hundred years ago, or even be further back in time. Relax and take your time. Let me know when you get there."

After a few minutes of silence, I noticed his eyelids fluttering. It looked as though he was scanning through time. Suddenly, his eyes steadied and calmed. He found what he was looking for.

He started to speak slowly. (To save time I have omitted much of the periods of silence between workds.) "I'm in uniform."

"Where are you?"

"In the Civil War... as a blue coat... but I'm fighting in the South. I'm looking around carefully ... I'm behind enemy lines."

"How old are you?"

"Young ... 20 or 21." All of a sudden, he yelled as if he were in pain and grabbed his chest moaning. "OW!"

"What's happening now?"

"I'm down under a bridge ... pain... shot in the chest. I can't walk ... I'm falling to the ground."

"You are okay. You can watch this scene as though it were a movie on a black-and-white television screen, which will lower the intensity of the experience."

His breathing slowly calmed down and he continued speaking. "I see a beautiful woman ... She heard the shot ... coming over to me. She's bending down and gently putting her finger to my lips and whispering, 'Don't try to speak.' She is using all her strength to drag me to the river just a few feet away

... She sighs relief as she gets me in the water ... I'm much lighter ... easier for her to move me around. She pulls me under the bridge where we can't be seen. I don't know why she is doing this ... She's a Reb." Then Michael fell silent.

"What's happening now?"

"She's holding me in her arms ... in the water ... out of the sight of the grey coats. I'm lying here ... bleeding ... bleeding." His voice trailed off; I had to lean in closer to hear him. "I feel very weak ... I look up at her deep blue eyes as she keeps watch."

"What is she wearing?"

"A sky-blue dress. It's floating in the water ... I feel the long flowing skirt surrounding me and touching me in the water ... I smell the sweetness of her skin. Mmm ... Her eyes are warm and loving." He moans.

"What's going on now?"

"Oh my God ... I'm dying in her arms." He went limp as he reconnected with the soldier's passing.

"Take a deep breath and allow this memory to pass. You can now let that life go." He took a deep breath and peace enveloped his face. "Take a few moments to feel the serenity from releasing the energy surrounding that life." I paused briefly to give him time to process, then continued. "When you are ready, let's go to another incarnation that has significance for you. Let me know when you get there."

"I'm Antonitus, a Roman centurion ... I lead armies into battle."

"Who did you do battle with?"

"The Philistines ... killed the King and allowed his daughter, Alexia, to live ... Didn't have the heart to kill her after she lay there ... weeping over her father's body." After a brief pause, he continued his narration.

"If the King's sword had not gotten stuck in the ground ... he would have thrust the sword right through me. Alexia is my captive, but I treat her as the princess she is ... never touched her out of lust or violence. I loved her, but never told her." His voice rang of regret and sorrow.

I had to keep him focused. "All right. Now let's go forward in that life time to when Antonitus passes on."

His eyes were moving rapidly under his eyelids. When they slowed down, he began to speak. "The night I drank the poisoned wine, Alexia was standing beside me." He turned toward me eyes still closed and asked, "Was it you, Alexia?"

I was confused.

"My God, it was, wasn't it?"

I ignored his reference to me as Alexia and asked, "Why did she kill you, Antonitus?"

"She loved me ... but she loved her father more," he gently sobbed. "And yet, she was so sad she poisoned me. I loved her ... so much. How could she do it?" He continued weeping.

He slowly lifted his head, and this time his eyes opened to meet my gaze, which startled me. Through his tear-soaked face he murmured, "The poison took hold of me; I died in her arms."

His eyes quickly closed again as he moaned and dropped off into silence.

I waited a few moments hoping to get a signal from him that he had processed this information. He did not stir. "Allow the feelings from that lifetime to drift away now. You are no longer there, and it no longer serves you. Go back to that space between lives and when ready, allow another lifetime that has significance for you to present itself."

He lay silent again.

I observed as his eyelids fluttered. Once his eyelids calmed, he was there. "I'm a pilot flying a B-17 in World War II ... shot down over Germany ... I am in a POW camp ... They didn't clean my wounds ... The deep gash in my arm was merely bandaged ... I was fed watery soup and potatoes. The interrogations were brutal. When they realized I was not going to give any valuable information, I was hung. He moaned in agony.

"What is happening now Michael?" I queried.

His hand was clutching his neck. "I feel the pain from the rope hanging around my neck."

"It's okay to feel it, but now you can allow it to dissipate. You can finally release the pain. It no longer serves you." The tension began to drain from his face, his shoulders relaxed.

"That's right Michael. You are safe and in the next few minutes you can come back into the room, taking what you need with you. You could, however, bring back any painful memories that would help you learn what you need for growth in your present life. Remember you could view them on a TV screen from a distance. I will count from one to five and you will be fully conscious and awake."

Michael opened his eyes. He looked as though he had been tossing and turning in his sleep all night. Tufts of hair turning every which way on his face. I offered him a glass of water. When he got acclimated back into the room, we discussed the session, looking for the common theme in each life.

"Michael, you were in battle in all three lives. Always a military man. In each life you suffered a great deal of physical pain and experienced violent deaths. Violence shrouded your life. On top of that, you were emotionally alone in each life."

"But Antonitus fell in love with Alexia," he countered.

"Yes, he loved her, but from a distance. There was no emotional involvement. No expression of those feelings." *Had he learned anything from these lives? Here I am falling in love with this guy. Is he emotionally unavailable? He seems to be in touch with my feelings but is he in touch with his own?*

The melancholy mood hung over me like a dense fog.

Out of the three past lives he accessed, Michael was obsessed with knowing about Antonitus and I admit, so was I.

During the next few months, our relationship continued to grow more intense and intimate. The physical attraction was undeniable. I got lost looking into his dreamy eyes and being held in his arms.

When he was off on weekdays, he met me at work at lunchtime. We drove to a nearby lake surrounded by a park. He picked up sandwiches, salads and dessert at a local deli. After lunch, we took a short walk around by lake before I had to head back to the office. Those days were light and fun.

Then, one evening, the circumstances took a turn. Michael came over after a late evening shift. He didn't want dinner, just some comfort food: coffee and oatmeal raisin cookies.

We were relaxing on the sofa listening to a Yanni tape. It was about one o'clock and I started to yawn. "I'm tired. C'mon hon, let's go upstairs to bed now."

His eyes turned to stone and his face turned cold. "No, you go upstairs," he said sternly. "I will sleep down here."

I was bewildered. "Why?"

"Because upstairs I'd be in your domain." He patted the sofa. "Down here it's mine. Now go!" he commanded, pointing to the stairs.

His tone of voice was totally alien to me. *What the hell is going on?*

He was glassy eyed, and his words were stiff. He looked at me in the strangest way, then tilted his head and said, "You are not beheaded yet?"

"Michael, what are you talking about?" I felt uneasy.

"You are only a woman; I am the master. I am a centurion."

"What's going on? Is this a joke?"

No response.

I took a deep breath and tried to calm myself down. "Okay, okay. I'll play along. What about compromise?"

"There is no compromise. It's my way or nothing!"

What's he talking about?

He continued his tirade. "Woman, how have you lived so long with such a loose tongue?"

I searched his face for laughter. There was none; his eyes were cold. I became unnerved. *Change the subject to divert his attention.*

"Did you talk to your ex-wife the way you are talking to me?"

"No," he replied coolly. "It's coming out now." He shoots me a contemptuous look. "It's your fault. You brought it out, now you will take it. When I say sleep, you will sleep, when I say eat, you will eat."

I couldn't believe what I was hearing. I felt goose bumps all over my body, so I covered up my fear by delivering a snappy retort. "I don't like the way you are talking to me. I think you should leave."

He scoffed. "No. I don't want to leave. In fact, I will not leave."

At this point I was so terrified I couldn't move or speak. For the first time, I felt the man in front of me was a total stranger. Maybe even dangerous. Then just as fast as this persona erupted, it faded.

His eyes fluttered, and the gentleness came back into his eyes. "What did I do, fall asleep? Come on honey, let's go to bed," he said softly.

I looked at him in disbelief. There was no telltale sign of a joke or knowledge for what had just happened. "Just a minute ago you told me to go upstairs alone." I searched his face for a reaction. There was none.

"No, I didn't," he replied seriously.

"Yes, you did." I explained what happened.

"You're kidding."

I studied his face. "I wish I were." A low-level fear was starting to creep up. What just happened seemed like an awful dream. I didn't want to admit to myself that something wasn't right. The red flag was there but I was in denial. I just witnessed Michael flashing back to Antonitus in the waking state while we were sitting and talking. *Was a part of Michael resurfacing from ancient times or is it possible there is another life form inhabiting Michael? Could there be another explanation?*

While occupied with my thoughts, Michael wrapped his arms around me and brushed his lips against my neck with a soft kiss. "C'mon, honey, it's going to be all right." He grabbed my hand and led me upstairs.

In the morning, I made breakfast and Michael went off to work. Last night's events weighed heavily on me. I didn't think there were beheadings in ancient Rome. I wondered if Michael got his time frames mixed up. After all, beheadings were introduced in England in the eleventh century. Shortly after Michael left, I did some research. I found that the Greeks and Romans did indeed perform beheadings, initially using an axe and eventually a sword.

The next time Michael came over, he was visibly tense. He flopped on the couch. "Kath, I've had a few rough days. We responded to a kitchen fire, but by the time we got there, the kitchen was pretty much destroyed. The owner did not have a fire extinguisher in the house. At least no one got hurt. We also had a bunch of building inspections. To make matters worse, I haven't slept well. Would you put on some Yanni music? It relaxes me."

Within minutes, Michael let out a deep sigh and closed his eyes. I reached over and began rubbing his temples and the back of his neck. Shortly thereafter, I snuggled in beside him. He seemed to doze off for a few minutes then reached over to give me a gentle kiss. Without hesitation he pulled me in tighter as he pressed his lips hard upon mine. I felt a shift and quickly opened my eyes. Michael's face had turned cold. I recognized the signs. He was switching again to Antonitus. He began speaking about himself in the third person.

"Is it wrong to only care about yourself and not others?" Antonitus snarled, not waiting for a response. "I don't think so. For the first time, I had fun with Michael. He went to do some building inspections and instead of him just giving them a warning, I made him give out $1,000 fines and tell two people to go f--- themselves." He threw back his head and let out a villainous laugh. "It felt good. I always wanted to do that."

As I watched his face in amazement, his eyes rolled under his lids again and he returned to normal. The Michael I knew had returned.

The evening's event put me into a panic. My head was spinning. *I need to think, but it's difficult with him around going in and out of Antonitus.* I looked at my watch. *He just got here a little while ago. Can't ask him to leave - he'll know something is wrong.*

"Michael, I forgot that I had to take my father to the doctor tomorrow for some tests. I'll be gone at least all morning. I'm so sorry it slipped my mind. You can come with us if you'd like."

"No, that's okay. I've got a few things I have to take care of. You take care of your dad."

Whew, just what I had hoped he would say.

When he left in the morning, I closed the door and collapsed on the couch. *What have I gotten myself into?* I called Gina.

"Why didn't you tell me about this earlier?" she demanded.

"I guess I wasn't thinking clearly." I felt like a petulant child being scolded.

"Something is not right here. I'm worried about you."

"I don't think he would hurt me."

"You don't know what he is capable of. Kath, you'd better get out of the relationship before it's too late."

The following Friday Michael was on his way over. An hour before he arrived, I paced the floor rehearsing what I was going to say.

When Michael opened the door, he leaned over to kiss me. I felt myself bristle but hoped he hadn't noticed.

"Get your jacket and pocketbook. We're going out to eat." He stood by the door.

I just want to tell him what I am feeling but now it would have to wait. He wanted to go to the movies, but I insisted we skip it. When we got back to the house, Michael shut the door. "Okay, what's going on? You barely touched your lunch and didn't want any dessert."

I braced myself. "Michael, I have been going over the events of the last few weeks. I think I have an idea about what's going on. It seems Antonitus is coming out through you intermittently in this life. His personality is bleeding through when he gets the opportunity. I suspect this has been happening to you for some time, but no one around you realized it. Your family and friends probably thought you were just moody. But I believe the real story is Antonitus is emerging in this life."

"Oh my God, Kathy! What are you saying? What have you done to me?" He paced the floor like a caged lion.

"Don't blame this on me. You must have met me for a reason. I think it has to do with this."

"This is crazy!" He threw his hands up in the air

"Think for a minute. Do you remember talking to Antonitus when you were a kid?"

"No, but I had an imaginary friend. So, what? Every kid does. It's no big deal."

"Yes, but I can't help but wonder. Maybe you were talking to Antonitus back then."

"How could you even think there's a connection? Kathy, back then, I knew what I was saying to my imaginary buddy. Here with you, I'm out like a light. I don't remember anything that Antonitus says to you. How do you explain that?"

"I don't know but that doesn't mean it never happened before you met me. How would you know, if you can't remember what you've said?"

Michael shrugged his shoulders.

"Exactly my point. When your eyes roll back that's a signal that your conscious mind is going under, and Antonitus is emerging. At times, I'm beginning to see Antonitus talk through you, without you going under. It seems like he's trying to push through more and more."

Michael listened intently, discomfort registering on his face.

"You have a difficult karma. Karma you created. Through the sessions and understanding Antonitus, it is clear you were heartless. Women were mere chattel. I believe Alexia felt it was her duty to kill Antonitus because he killed her father. Besides, he was so ruthless, she did everyone a favor by getting rid of him."

Since there was no response, I continued. "It seems to me that through many lifetimes, opportunities were presented to you so that you could raise the vibration of your spirit and help your fellow man. You were a Roman centurion, a leader of the people. Instead you chose to take advantage of that power. On the other hand, you were a pilot in World War II and a soldier in the Civil War defending your country and the right of people to be free. In this life you save people in fires, which fills a need for you. Michael, you need the adrenaline rush. You need that sense of power and control - that feeling of holding your own life, and the lives of others, in your hands, and cheating death. In fact, sometimes it seems you enjoy the seduction of violence and fear. I don't think saving lives make up for the violence."

He was speechless.

Realizing what I had just said, fear enveloped me. How was Michael going to react? Part of me wanted to run, but I couldn't. There seemed to be an invisible force field that kept me captivated, and I truly cared for Michael. I wanted to resolve the issue to set him free.

"Michael, don't you see, the closer you and I become, more information surfaces? It feels like we are breaking into another dimension together. One that transcends time and space."

He stared at the floor. "It's so surreal, I don't know what to say."

When Michael left, I poured myself a glass of wine and slumped on the couch. As exhausted as I was, I couldn't relax. The intrigue and fear kept racing in my head. I sensed danger but couldn't stop myself from delving deeper. I wanted to find out what Antonitus needed to be at peace and, let Michael live his own life. Of course, my motive wasn't entirely altruistic; I wanted to fit into that equation by Michael's side. With that aspiration, I finally fell into a deep sleep.

Monday morning, I woke up to the phone ringing. Initially, I thought it was the alarm clock because it was a work-day. I glanced at the time; it was only 5:15 a.m. It was Gina.

"Is everything okay?"

"Oh yeah. Didn't mean to startle you but I wanted to catch you before you jumped in the shower and run off to work. There is something on my mind. So I'm just going to say it. Kath, we hardly get together anymore. You work most of the time now and whatever free time you have, you spend with your boyfriend. I'm feeling like I'm losing my best friend."

"Gina, you are still my best friend. No one can replace you. It's just that I'm trying to figure out what is going on with Michael and Antonitus and it is consuming me."

"Yes, I know. So that's why I want to know if you want to blow off work today. We can go shopping, eat out and whatever else you want to do. What do you say?"

I felt remorseful. "You know, you are right. I need to turn off my brain for a while. We need a day just you and me. Let's do it!"

Michael and I agreed there had to be a way to outsmart Antonitus. We agreed to steadily move forward pursuing Antonitus to seek answers. In a subsequent session, while Michael was under, Antonitus surfaced. " I long to talk with Alexia. Could you bring her out?" He recited a poem for Alexia.

When Michael came out of hypnosis, I told him about the poem.

"What was it about?" he asked.

"I can't remember. I was so taken by it. In our next session, I'll ask Antonitus if he remembers it."

As usual, before our next session, Michael asked me to put on Yanni music. After Michael was in trance, I asked Antonitus to repeat the beautiful poem he had recited last time he spoke. The tape recorder was close at hand.

As he began repeating the poem aloud, I hit the record button. It made a clicking sound and stopped. Something was wrong, and it wasn't taping. I began fidgeting with it, making a lot of noise trying to get it going. Michael opened his eyes, but it was Antonitus who appeared, distracted and irritated. He looked around for the cause of the racket. His eyes settled on the recorder. "What is that?"

"A tape recorder," I responded, feverishly trying to get it to run before the trance was lost.

"A tape?"

"Yes, it records what you say." He looked puzzled. " In a way, the tape recorder writes down everything you say and keeps it so that you can listen to it when you want to. It's like reading a book, only you hear it instead of read it."

"Oh," he replied, but still looked confused.

All the while, I was still trying to get the recorder going, but to no avail. The trance was lost. Michael came back to the present. "What happened?"

"I can't get the recorder to work. I guess my fidgeting with it took you out of trance."

"But I want to hear the poem. Give me that damn thing, I'll fix it." Within a few moments it was working again. "I'm ready, bring me back." Michael sat back in the chair and closed his eyes.

Once he was in, I asked, "Antonitus, would you recite the poem for me again?"

Annoyance was displayed on his face. "Did it fall on deaf ears the first time?" He opened his eyes briefly, threw me a steely-eyed look and quickly closed them.

"No." I had to think fast. "It was so lovely; I want to hear it again."

A warm smile blanketed his face as he began reciting:

"Mountains high, rivers flow, skies are blue, beckon to me.
Restless souls keep on turning, spending life being free.
It's a perfect day, the sun is shining, I wish that you could share it with me.
No matter what I do, I just can't get you off my mind.
You're everywhere I go, everywhere I know.
You're everything I see. I don't know what's happened to me.
I can't get you off my mind."

He paused then asked: "Is it tonight Alexia?"

I didn't have the foggiest idea what he was referring to but played along. "No."

"But," he sighed, "it is you. All this time, I've wanted you." While in trance, he reached out, pulled me close and gave me a passionate kiss then pushed me away. "But I would not have you because then, destiny would change."

"How so?"

"If I make love to you, you will not kill me. You would want to be with me even though I ran my sword through your father. If I had to do it over, I would do the same thing. I told you, I have killed over and over without any feelings. But when I plunged that sword into your father's heart, and saw your face, something inside me was ripped apart. Maybe it was because of my love for you. And, I knew you would hate me when you found out what I did." He put his head into his hands as he shook it back and forth. "My God, I wish he had enough strength to put his sword into me."

"Could you run that steel through my body?" I asked.

"No," he said vehemently. "I would stop steel for you. I would make you my queen, if I could." He paused.

Antonitus appeared melancholy and remorseful. Maybe in his moment of weakness it was a good time to question him.

"Antonitus, why do you stay with Michael?"

"We are good for each other."

"How so?"

"He needs the push. On the outside he looks strong and tough. Inside he's a loving person, but without me, he doesn't have the strength to go and fight."

"Why does he have to fight? Can't he just love?"

He scoffed. "Love does not put bread on the table, woman. Besides, he loves being a firefighter. I love it too. He does a lot of gutsy moves."

"And those moves almost took his life a few times," I added.

"I was there," assured Antonitus. "I made sure nothing happened to him. I remember one time when a wall collapsed and came down on him. It came down on me too. His legs were pinned down, but he had enough strength to inch his way out. He couldn't have done that without me. He needed my strength and will to keep going."

"But don't you keep him from getting into a loving relationship, much like you from Alexia?"

He ignored my question. "When he wants something, he goes for it and I hardly come out. I know about you. You're Kath."

"Yes."

"Michael loves you very much."

"He may, but I think you have a big influence on him and you could make him walk away from our relationship at any time. It is to your advantage to keep him isolated from other people so that you can control him. You are cold."

"I'm cold?" he replied with impish amusement.

"Yes."

He relented. "Indeed, I'm the cold one; he is passionate and loving."

I pushed him to say more. "So, you want him to walk away, don't you?"

"He walks away when I tell him to walk away. I could make him quit his job and be a mamma's boy if need be. Or a housewife, if I tell him so."

I was annoyed at his arrogance but kept my composure. After all, I didn't know what he was capable of. I wasn't getting anywhere so I decided to take a different tact. "What would he do for me?"

There was a pause; he moaned as he casually tapped his fingers together. "I feel he would do almost anything for you, as

I, for Alexia. But truth be told, I have not had Alexia the way I wanted to."

"But you could have Alexia through Michael."

He scoffed. "It's not the same! There's part of you in there. I want Alexia. She was my true love. All these years I've yearned for her."

"Are not Alexia and I the same woman?"

"No! Besides, I'm sure Michael wants just you. Imagine four people at one time in only two bodies."

"Yes, but I think ..." He cuts me off.

"No! Stars would fall from the sky. The heavens would open. Maybe, just maybe, the sun would not shine the next day."

Oh God! He's so melodramatic. "Well then, when Michael wants to make love to Kath are you going to leave him alone?"

"If he wants," Antonitus said coyly. "Or, if you want. Woman, you can ask me now. I will allow it. Come, Kath. ASK ME!" he demanded.

I shot him a glance. "Ask you what?"

"Ask me if I'm going to leave him alone for you!"

I was annoyed with his banter. He was engaging me in a power play and forcing me to submit. He was the cat, I was the mouse. I acquiesced. "Okay. Now, will you leave him alone?"

"Yes, if you want me to, I will. Let him take over everything. Let him figure things out for himself." He snickered. "He'll be lost without me. He'll be weak, like a woman."

I ignored his pointed remark. "Antonitus, who were you kissing before?"

"My princess, the only one I ever loved, truly loved. She poisoned me, Kath. Oh God, I stuck a sword right into her father's heart, and for that I am forever sorry." His voice was grief-filled as it trailed off to a whisper. He sighed and took a moment to regain his composure. "Something deep inside got to me after the battle. I took her rather than have her killed because she was a princess. Her beauty inside and out moved me like never before. I kept her alive. I could have put her head on a platter anytime I wanted to. She was so beautiful, and because of my love for her I was so vulnerable. I knew she wanted to kill me and still, I allowed it to happen. I drank the poisoned wine."

"Why?" I prodded.

"I felt guilt. She would never have truly loved me because of her father. So, I had no reason to live."

He was a master at being elusive. "Getting back to my question, will you allow Michael to love Kathy completely? With passion and openness, the way a man should love a woman? Will you allow him that, so he can be free and really love someone?"

"If he wants," Antonitus repeated dryly.

My gut told me he was lying. "Do you think he wants to?"

Antonitus hesitated. "It's hard for him, but yes, he does. You can have your wish. He will not be hearing from me anymore.

I will leave Michael now. He is in good hands. I have finally found the person who will keep him safe."

He seemed so lost and lonely I almost felt sorry for him. I had to remind myself that Antonitus was playing me.

The tape recorder started clicking because it came to the end of the tape. The clicking startled Michael out of trance. He looked around as if he had just woken up from a deep sleep. My eyes searched his face. "Do you remember what just happened?"

"All I remember is asking you to put on the Yanni tape because it relaxes me." He took a deep breath and stretched his arms.

"Don't you remember Antonitus talking?"

"No." he seemed totally unaware.

"Antonitus and I had a long conversation. It would have continued but the damn recorder started making noise and you snapped out of it. Here, let me play it for you."

Michael listened intently to the tape. "I recognize the poem." He stopped the tape. "It's actually part of a song from the seventies. How could Antonitus know it?"

"My guess is he is able to access and use any information that you know because you share the same consciousness. The bleed through could go both ways, from past lives to present and present to past lives." I turned the tape back on.

Michael was unemotional until he heard Antonitus was going to leave him alone to live his own life. His eyes welled up with tears.

"What's wrong?" I asked.

"He's gone forever. I feel it. I feel like I lost a part of me that I've had my whole life."

"Don't you think it's about time?"

"You don't understand. How am I going to fight fires now? I need him. You heard him. He was my push. I need him."

"Michael, no you don't. He was that angry part of you that lashed out at everyone and everything. He's the part that got you into trouble. He's gone and that's good. Don't you see? You are free to live your life in peace. To live happily ever after. This is wonderful. I think this is the best thing that could have happened."

"What do you mean?"

"I think you were healed of a bleed through, or kind of personality split you have been dealing with. It was as though two people shared the same body. I believe he took over and ruled your mind. He was probably living inside of you all along."

In the next few days, I felt Antonitus was gone completely. Although part of me would miss our connection, I was happy to be free of him especially when Michael was no longer switching.

Two weeks later, just as I was getting used to thinking Antonitus had become a memory, he came back, appearing more frequently. Once again, reality became more complicated. We were sitting talking, and suddenly, I saw that familiar eye roll on Michael.

"You thought you got rid of me," Antonitus said with an icy stare.

"Yes." I was really shaken.

"Well, you can't get rid of me."

"But you said you were leaving," I added, trying to hide the fear and disappointment in my voice.

"And you believed me, you foolish girl. I can't leave Michael. Without me, he would die. He's weak; I am his backbone. He has so many problems, without me he would give up."

"What problems Antonitus?"

The silence was deafening. In a flash his eyes rolled, and Michael returned, unaware of what had just occurred. He looked at the horror in my face and knew. "Kathy, what's wrong? Oh my God. He's back isn't he?"

"Sadly, yes."

With that, he panicked and turned on me. "This is all your fault! You brought out this monster in me." He pointed his finger. "I was fine until I met you!"

"Calm down Michael! You know that's not true. We've been through this conversation before. You admitted you know he is your adrenaline when you go into fires. You acknowledged his presence when you have gotten angry and did violent things. You are scared and lashing out at me."

"Maybe that's true."

"In fact, I believe he has been coming in and out of you as needed, and you weren't even aware of it. So, don't blame me. The way I see it, I was just able to identify what has been happening all along."

"Okay, okay," conceded Michael. "But what are we going to do about him?"

"I don't know. I'm working on it. I'm trying to get him to leave for good, but he has a strong hold on you. Your attachment to him isn't helping either. Look, let's shelve it for the rest of today. I can't think anymore."

We had a glass of wine and fell asleep on the couch. The next morning, Michael kissed me awake. We playfully began wrestling, and before you know it, we were kissing heavily. At one point, he tightened his grip with his left arm around my neck and right hand around my head as he pressed his lips hard against mine. It was out of character for Michael. Excitement shot right down to my pubis. I opened my eyes. Just as I thought. It was Antonitus.

"Antonitus, is that you?"

Coyly, he answered, "You know it is, Kathy."

He was right. I did know it was him. He kissed me again. God, what passion! I melted into his arms, moaning with pleasure. I didn't want him to stop!

"Kathy, I want to make love to you," Antonitus cooed.

I wanted that too, but it didn't feel right. I sat up. "I can't make love to you. Michael would be angry," I reasoned.

"TO HELL with Michael! He is a boy, and I, a man. I will buy you from Michael. You are worth at least a thousand drachmas. But first, I will make unbridled love to you like you've never had before." He pulled me into his chest and started kissing my neck, inching his way up to my lips. He lifted my arm and kissed it slowly, starting from my hand passionately all the way up to my armpit, sending chills up and down my body. "Such a sweet aroma," he murmured. He started kissing my ear while he opened my blouse. He felt my bra, and puzzled, looked down at it. "What is this cloth that binds you?" he asked as he pulled it down, exposing my breasts.

"My bra," I answered not wanting him to stop kissing me.

"How silly." He dismissed it and continued kissing my body. I melted. His hands evoked electricity wherever he placed them. I wanted him to rip my clothes off when he stopped abruptly. His face changed; he was back to Michael. He looked aghast at the passion on my face.

"Oh my God! He's doing this to you! That bastard! And you were going along with it! How could you?" He jumped up walking across the room.

"Michael, wait." I started buttoning my blouse. "You're acting like I'm kissing another man! Like I'm cheating on you. I'm not. At least I don't think so because that other man is you.

What am I supposed to do? Tell him to leave me alone? God, I'm so confused. Weren't you there when he was kissing me?"

"No. I don't remember anything," he replied coldly.

"Well, I can't take much more of this back and forth stuff. At first it was intriguing, but now it's getting too damn weird."

Sometimes when I'm totally involved in my own myopic world, I don't see the big picture until one day it crystallizes. I thought about Michael's switching back and forth to Antonitus and something he said nonchalantly on our first date: "Viola, has been giving me a hard time about seeing my daughter. She is just a bitch and she's done whatever she could to make me miserable. I really miss Kitty." I felt that when Michael was ready, he would tell me the whole story. That time never came. What was it that he had so neatly hidden? Could it be a clue to what was going on? Next time we are going to be together, I will find out.

"Michael, have you been open and honest with me about everything?" I queried.

"Of course."

"Well, I remember early on you inferred you haven't seen Kitty for a while. Would you tell me why?"

"I didn't want to bother you with it, but if you really want to know, I'll tell you."

"I do. If it's important to you, it is to me."

"Okay. I told you I was married up until four years ago. When Vy told me she wanted a divorce, I got angry and started throwing things around the house. After that, she took out a Writ of Protection against me because I had angry outbursts. Kath, my ex-wife was a spiteful bitch and that's why I have no visitation rights. On top of all that, she had my daughter testify in court against me; accusing me of inappropriate sexual behavior. This was an outright lie! Vy was extremely cunning to pull this off. I had fits of anger but there was no sexual inappropriateness with my daughter."

I gave him a sympathetic glance.

"I'm telling you my ex coached my daughter to get back at me. How could she turn Kitty against me like that? How sick! I don't know how she brainwashed her. I can't stand her for doing that. Kath, I didn't do it. I swear to God. My heart has been breaking because I have not been allowed to see my daughter since we separated." Michael looked devastated. "The only reason she is still alive is because she is the mother of my child," he uttered.

As he said those words, I watched him clench his fists. I shuddered. *It's tough to orchestrate a whole story like that even to the point where the daughter swore in court she was touched inappropriately by her father when she wasn't. From what Michael told me, Karen explained things in a sexual way that a child her age would not know how to explain unless she had experienced them. However, on the other hand, Children are pliable. Could she have been coached so well that she was convincing when she testified in court? Maybe she was just saying a bunch of words that were memorized, not really knowing the impact of that testimony.* I felt a queasiness deep down in my stomach.

If Michael turned into Antonitus he may have been capable of such debauchery. Dare I say what I was thinking? Would I be the thorn bird that finally impales itself upon the thorn bush? There was no polite way to brooch the subject. Was I taking a chance with my safety? By the following weekend, I had to say it to see the reaction on his face. "Michael, do you think it's possible that when you were living at home with your wife and daughter, you turned into Antonitus once when you were alone with Kitty and, well, he behaved inappropriately? That would explain why you were unaware of it and Kitty was so convincing in front of the judge." As my words sank into his head, he froze then began to cry. Tears were streaming down his face.

"If I did that to my daughter," Michael screamed in agony, "I'll cut these hands off." He looked down at them with disgust and hatred. His wailing became louder. "I would never hurt her!" Michael was lost in a river of tears and pain.

I was petrified he would do something stupid to himself or me. After all, the Writ of Protection is proof that underneath his calm demeanor was a raging temper. Could this man have a personality disorder? It didn't even matter at this point what

the cause was. I was treading in dangerous territory. Every part
of me was telling me to run. I felt like I just poked a beehive.

For the first time, I admitted to myself that I had to find a
way out of this relationship unscathed. The joy I felt with him
had turned to sheer terror. "Michael, forget what I said! It's
ridiculous! I'm sorry. I'm sure you aren't capable of violence. I
was just searching for something that would make sense."

We never again discussed the elephant in the room, but the
thought of Michael committing such an egregious crime made
my blood run cold. Was my fear real or imagined? After all, he
wasn't violent with me. Maybe, I didn't know Michael at all. If
he truly molested his daughter to any degree, then he should be
behind bars. But, I had no hard proof and no way of knowing
for sure what the truth was. I cannot say Antonitus was real or
imagined. People under hypnosis can access past lives or
hidden memories. They can also create a fictitious story which
their resourceful mind fabricated to bring attention to an
underlying theme in their life for healing purposes.

Throughout the coming weeks, I tried to act as though
things were back to normal especially since Antonitus was quiet
again. But I knew Antonitus was shrewd. At this point, I had
little hope that he would leave Michael in peace. Whatever the
case, I knew for sure it was time to exit from the relationship. I
had to outsmart the fox. And, it had to be subtle.

So began the subterfuge. "Michael, my part time practice is picking up and if I want it to grow, I have to devote more time to it. I have to set appointments after work in the evening and weekends."

"What about us?" he argued.

I gently touched his arm and feigned a sorrowful look. "It won't be easy for me too. If it becomes a full practice, then I can quit my day job."

"Yeah, but how long before that happens?"

"I should have a better idea within six months or a year."

Michael shrugged his shoulders. "What can I say? I'm not happy about it."

In the following weeks, we saw each other a few times. Our phone calls were short because I said I had clients arriving. Michael needed a lot of attention and he wasn't getting it. He began to recoil. I was careful, so he didn't think I was afraid, or didn't want to be with him. It was a delicate balance.

One day, he sat me down and said, "Kathy, I barely get to see you anymore. When I am around, you're preoccupied with work."

I mustered up as much sincerity as I could and apologized. "I'm sorry. I'm frazzled from working all the time."

"Maybe, we should take a break from each other for a while. See how it feels."

"Whatever you think Michael." **He bought it.** My heart was racing. "If that is what you really want, I suppose we should try it." I hid my jubilation.

"For a while" became six months, then a year. I kept thinking, "too easy." For quite some time, I was looking over my shoulder, expecting him to show up without warning, wanting to get back together, or so angry that he would harm me.

In retrospect, I realize the biggest thing we had in common was our fascination for Antonitus. We were drawn together by this strange past life. Although it was exciting, it made Michael mercurial. Besides, it was getting dangerous. My one regret was that we were unsuccessful in uprooting Antonitus. Perhaps he had a terrible childhood and Antonitus was a way he devised to cope. A few times, I had suggested he talk to a therapist, but he denied he needed one.

Michael said he wanted his life to go back to normal, or what he perceived as normal before he met me. He didn't want to think about the possibility that he may have behaved inappropriately with his daughter. That was too painful. Did he do it or was he innocent? I'll never know.

Although I wish him peace and happiness, somehow, I imagine Antonitus continues to make appearances and to control Michael. I kept his phone number in my wallet, occasionally feeling tempted to call to find out what was going on in his life.

I hadn't heard from him for a few years. It was as though he had dropped off the face of the earth. Finally, I felt at ease that whatever had transpired between us, was over.

One day, as I was walking, I searched for the piece of paper in my purse with his telephone number. I stared at it for the very last time before I ripped it up into little pieces and watched as the wind swept it away. Now, I was totally free.

PART V

Comfort and Confirmation

Chapter 25

Janie

Janie had acid reflux, which caused the back of her vocal chords and throat to burn, resulting in a raspy voice. The doctor prescribed medication and said it would take several months to regain her voice. She cleared her throat and popped a lozenge in her mouth. "I can only whisper, and it hurts to talk. I took some of your classes at a local college. One really resonated with me, *Forgiveness: The Key to Inner Peace*. Forgiveness has been an unattainable goal for me. After hearing you speak, I felt you could help me."

"What happened prior to the symptoms?"

"My mother had passed away three years earlier from Alzheimer's – a devastating event for all of us. During her illness, my father became increasingly angry and unsympathetic. He was even embarrassed to be seen with her. I couldn't understand it." She shrugged her shoulders.

"What are your feelings toward your father?" I prodded.

"Ugh," she snarled. I couldn't stand being in his presence. I found myself wishing he was the one with Alzheimer's. Every time I was near him, I wanted to vomit. I got this feeling down in my stomach and then back up my throat." She made a motion of her fist turning, curling, and moving down into her stomach and back up again to her throat.

"Wait a minute, let's back up. Did you see what you just did?"

Janie stared blankly. "No. What did I do?"

"Look at the motion you just showed me." I mirrored it back to her.

"Oh my God!" She grabbed her stomach. "I realize WHY I was feeling the way I did. WHY I didn't have a voice. The acid reflux and lost voice were real, but the cause was from not being able to 'swallow' what my father did to my mother."

She got it. All I had to do was show her.

Tears rolled down her face.

"It's okay to feel upset, as long as you release it. Holding it in is can get us sick. We are going to use the Emotional Freedom Technique (EFT), which combines tapping on certain meridian points while saying 'even though I have this anger for my father, I totally and completely love and accept myself.' Let's do a few rounds together." We tapped on other feelings as they arose.

Janie felt a shift. "I feel some pressure was released. I guess my father was struggling with loneliness and helplessness. He didn't know how to handle the stress."

"That's a wonderful insight, Janie. Continue to use the tapping on this or anything else. If another feeling arises, tap on that too. It's like peeling the layers of an onion."

Within a week of practicing EFT, her voice started to come back. Within two weeks, it was completely normal. She called to tell me the good news. Her ENT was VERY surprised her voice came back so quickly. He never would have believed what worked, so she didn't tell him.

We both laughed. "I guess that'll be our little secret."

Chapter 26

Annette

While walking with some friends in the woods of the beautiful Ramapo Mountains, located in southeastern Rockland County, we decided to take a break. One of the women, Annette, said she had always been agnostic. Now, everyone holding hands, sitting in a healing circle, Annette said for the first time she saw and felt energy. Annette had a slight limp and feeling safe in the group, she decided to share intimate details. "I was born with congenital defects that affected my gait. Doctors thought I may have had polio as a baby. I always wanted to believe I could be healed and walk normally like everyone else."

Moved by her admission, I knelt down in front of Annette and channeled energy into her right foot and leg, then finished with a soft, gentle massage.

"My God Kathy, my mom used to massage my leg when I was a child. It feels different though. I know you are working on me out of love, but my mother did it out of obligation, and guilt." Annette let out a heartfelt sigh. "There was hardly any other physical contact with my mother except for an occasional peck on the cheek."

"Many of us have childhood experiences that affect our lives. Forgiving your mother will help you more than anything else."

"It's difficult."

"It usually is, but it's worth it."

Months later, I received a call from Annette. "Kath, I have news. The day you worked on me, I felt hopeful. I have been cultivating patience and understanding for my mom, although some days are still difficult. Also, within a few days, I realized my foot wasn't bothering me as much as usual and I could push myself past my physical limit without a lot of pain. Now here is the exciting part." Her voice was melodic and joyful. "Since I was a little girl, I dreamed of being a dancer. I thought that would never happen. However, after the healing session with you, I took ballroom dance lessons and danced in the spotlight in front of a hundred people. I know now there is healing energy and that you, Kathy, are a conductor of that energy."

Chapter 27

Victor and Coleen

Victor did not freak out over twenty years ago when I started seeing deceased relatives around him because growing up his Aunt Marie saw spirits around people, and he saw ghosts in his childhood home. About four years ago, he asked me to do a reading for his wife, Coleen, who had just lost her 41-year-old brother, Tim, to cancer. They were close, and she was having a difficult time with his passing.

"Vic, I don't usually try to read people - they just appear when they want to. I don't know if anyone would come through if I ask them to."

"You can do it, I know you can!"

Reluctantly, I agreed to do the reading that week. Spirit usually gave me something to tell the person that I would not have known unless it was communicated to me. Although I received information while reading Coleen, it wasn't unique. I asked Tim to give me something that would validate his presence. In my mind's eye he showed me an ID bracelet. I offered the information to Coleen. She gasped. "I usually wear an ID bracelet that contains his ashes inside, but I took it off a few weeks ago."

"My feeling is he brought it up to validate that he is with you and he would like you to wear it again."

Chapter 28
Lynn

Walking through the hall at work, I overheard a woman, Lynn, talking about her teenage son who had died a few months earlier. Feeling the pain and sorrow in her voice, I approached her.

"I couldn't help but overhear your conversation about your son. I'm sorry. It must be so difficult for you."

"It is, but thanks for your kind words."

"I have a feeling that your son is fine. Except he misses his family terribly."

She smiled faintly.

"Has anything odd happened since he died?"

Lynn looked surprised. "Yes. In fact, I have felt my son's presence. I even felt him touch my hand." She gently caressed one hand over the other. "He was a wonderful soul. A great inspiration to his peers. Very bright, motivated and always optimistic despite having Muscular Dystrophy."

A few days later, I called her on the phone.

"Lynn, do you have a minute?"

"Sure."

"I know this is going to sound strange, but I received a message from your son. He wants me to tell you that without his physical body, he can really soar like an eagle."

Lynn started to cry but quickly gained her composure. "I'd really like to talk to you, but I would rather speak in person."

We made plans to meet for lunch.

"Kathy, what you said meant so much to me and here's why. My son, Stephen, was eighteen, 48 pounds, and wheelchair bound when he died. Every day, my husband used to tell him, 'Son, you really make my heart soar like an eagle.' So, when you gave me the message, it was specific and meaningful. I can't thank you enough."

A few weeks later, Lynn stopped by my office. She sat down and began to tell me how much she missed her son. As she was talking, I saw an image of Stephen in back of her. Listening to what he was telling me, I had to interrupt her.

"Lynn, it's difficult to hear what you are saying because your son is here. He's talking softly and I'm trying to listen. He's standing very close to you."

"Really?" She looked around the room. "What's he saying?"

"He's jiggling up and down because he is so excited that he can communicate with you through me."

"Oh my gosh! He always jiggled up and down when he got excited!"

"Now he's showing me something white. It's made of cotton. I think it's a shirt. No, it's too small to be a shirt. It's only a few inches wide."

"The other day, I was in his room and found one white glove from when he was Mickey Mouse at Halloween when he was four years old. I looked all over and couldn't find the other one. That must be it," she bellowed with nervous excitement. "It's the glove!"

"I think he is letting you know he was in the room with you, watching when you found the glove. Now he is showing me a place where there are very tall trees. He told me he loved this place. Does that mean anything to you?"

"Yes, we took him to Muir Woods, California; he loved the redwoods. It was one of his favorite places."

I continued receiving information. "Now he is showing me when you were younger. I see you with long curly hair, and Stephen sitting next to you, twirling your hair."

A warm smile washed over her face. "He loved to do that."

At that point I couldn't hold back the emotion I was feeling and broke down and cried, wiping the tears from my face. I was the bridge between them feeling their love and the pain of them being apart.

Lynn grabbed my hand. "It's okay."

Through my tears, I started to laugh. "This is really funny Lynn, you're comforting me!"

"Kathy, you have to understand. Now I know Stephen is okay - hearing from him has been a great comfort."

Chapter 29

Deidra

After the morning meditation at the ashram with Baba Shivarudra Balayogi Maharaj, a yogi from India, there was a short break. As I was stretching, my arm bumped into the woman next to me. We chuckled.

"My name is Deidra," she said, extending her hand.

As soon as we connected, a vision appeared. "Mine's Kathy." Without a moment's delay, I blurted out, "By the way, what's with all the roses around you?"

Startled, she stepped back, her hand on her chest. "There's a story behind that. About ten years ago, my mother gave my husband Joe and I a rose bush to plant in our yard. It never bloomed all these years. It's not my garden soil because I have lots of other red, pink and coral rose bushes that bloom beautifully. As I was leaving two days ago to come here, I looked at the unopened buds and said, 'when I get back next week, let's throw it out.' Well my husband called this morning to tell me the bush has a few blooms!"

Five days later Deidra called. "You won't believe this. I just got home from the ashram and waiting for me were three vases filled with roses from my mother's bush!" I never got a chance to say goodbye to my mother, but I think the blossoming bush was a sign. I feel like a piece of my heart was healed."

Chapter 30

Sue

Working in the distance learning side of a college, I handled occasional student issues. I had to meet with Sue because of a discrepancy in the class she signed up for. Upon coming face-to-face with her, I felt queasy and in my mind's eye, saw a written letter. After the class issue was resolved, I mentioned my finding. "We've never met before, so this is going to sound strange, but I'm getting the feeling there has been a lot of death around you."

"How did you know that?"

"I get these feelings along with visions. Also, I feel there is a letter that has a lot of significance for you."

She shook her head.

I was sure. "The feeling is strong. It could be a letter from years ago."

Deep in thought, her face suddenly froze. "The day my son Brian was killed in a car accident, he had written me a letter before he drove away. He said he loved me and promised that he would return home. He died that night and the letter was the last communication I had with him."

She pulled a tissue out of her purse and wiped her face. "I've been waiting years, since my son's passing, to hear from him. I paid a lot of money to psychics, but no one was able to tell me anything. You may have felt death around me because Brian died 15 years ago, and I have never recovered. I lost my dad when I was five years old and a year and a half later my grandfather, who helped rear me after my father passed."

"I feel like your son got caught up in some kind of community that was not good for him."

"He did. He was involved in rave concerts - crazy, wild huge dance parties. Most used the drug ecstasy. They wore baby pacifiers around their necks supposedly so when doing drugs, they would not bite their tongues. Followers went all around the country to these concerts."

"I'm sure he regrets it. He says he is sorry for all the things that he did and the pain he caused you. He knows he drove you crazy. He also says the situation at home had nothing to do with him making bad decisions." I looked at Sue. "Does that make sense?"

"Yes. His dad and I separated and there was a lot of upheaval. Arguments. Stress."

"Now I see these big, rock-like things. I'm not sure what they are. Any idea?"

"Oh my God. Yes. Brian had these huge heavy mushrooms made out of plaster of Paris." They stand about three feet tall. We have them in the backyard." She laughed. "Every time I move, they come with me."

"Now I see an older man who has passed on who loved his carbs. What's with the needles?"

"Oh, that's my grandfather, he was diabetic. I used to watch him give himself needles morning and evening. And yes, he did love his carbs. He had his shredded wheat and grapefruit and prunes every morning." Sue chuckled. "Died from complications of diabetes."

"Okay, well he's with your son now."

"I'm so glad," Sue smiled.

"Was Brian tall and thin with dark hair?"

"No. that was my dad."

"I mixed them up because they were together, and they can appear younger than when they passed. He says, 'tell her I'm watching out for Brian because he needs watching after.'"

Sue let out a howl. "True, true!"

"Now I'm hearing the words, tears of a clown. Any significance?"

"No."

The following day Sue and I talked by phone.

"I'm glad you were able to give me the reading, but I have to be honest. When I went home last night I looked at Brian's picture and said, 'why didn't you send me something that was hard and fast to make me believe without a doubt that it was you?'"

I was feeling her disappointment when I heard a voice in my head. "Mention the bananas." *That sounds ridiculous. I can't repeat that.* The voice was adamant. "**Ask about the bananas!**"

"Sue, this sounds really weird, but I hear a voice telling me to mention the bananas."

She started to cry. "I can't believe it. There is no way you could make that up. Me and a friend went to a place called Common Ground and had banana smoothies. At home, I made them with Brian who became obsessed with them. He loved them so much he had to have them every day. The bananas had to be frozen, then pureed. My dream is to someday open a little coffee shop on Cape Cod named Uncle Brian's Banana Smoothies where the smoothies would be featured. So, for you to hear, ask about the bananas, was a true confirmation for me." She let out a long, deep, audible breath.

Two weeks later she called, her voice was filled with excitement. "Kath remember you mentioned the tears of a clown?"

"Yes."

"At first I didn't get it, but Brian's grandmother had this porcelain music box of a clown who sings "send in the clowns." His head was tipped to the side and there were tears dripping down the side of his face. When Brian went to her house, he'd wind it up and listen to it for hours. He loved it so much that eventually his grandmother gave it to him. I have to tell you, I am so relieved knowing he is okay. As a matter of fact, I went to the cemetery and told him I'm feeling much better now. I'm no longer fighting the daily sadness. Kath, I told the whole family what you did. Your insight has helped all of us. I finally feel at peace."

PART VI

Channeling

Channeling

For twenty years I had a meditation group at my house once a month. Some people attended for a few weeks, others stayed for many years. Each time before the group met, I meditated on each person and oftentimes received messages for them. On occasion, spirit had a sense of humor and delivered funny messages, other times, I was urged to give a collective message for the group. I believe these messages were given from tapping into my higher consciousness, which is connected to a universal consciousness - free from frailty, prejudice and ill will. When the messages are heard, they convey a lesson or promote a sense of peace and balance. Although they were conveyed within a small meditation circle, I believe they are applicable to a more global audience. Below are a few of those messages that were delivered to the group. The first one is my favorite.

The Ego

This ego that masquerades as my dearest friend is truly my most cunning, shrewd enemy. Its advantage is knowing all of my weaknesses. It knows how to twist my strengths so that I perceive them as weaknesses. It knows what I'm thinking, so it knows how to sabotage my next move. It's like a vine choking a bush, squeezing all life from it until it turns a pale gray. How does one defeat such an enemy? What chance does one have at victory?

There is but one opportunity to defeat the power of this indefatigable enemy. It is simple yet difficult. It can be vanquished in an instant or many lifetimes. I can give you the key to overcome this beast, but if you blink you may not see it, if you do not listen carefully, you may not hear it, if you do not think about it you may not understand it. The truth, revealed from the book, A Course In Miracles, (ACIM) is that the ego makes us think we are separate from God; it is out to destroy our peace of mind. It keeps its power over us by keeping us in this illusion of separateness. Once we see this, the spell is broken and we may begin to live our lives in balance and harmony. Like anything else, practice is needed to keep it fresh in our minds.

The Creator

God has many gifts to give us. We just have to be able to accept them. Oftentimes we feel unworthy to receive. Allow healing to come in on any level it deems to be necessary, whether physical, emotional and/or spiritual. Know that all of your sins have been forgiven and it is your birthright to be happy. At this moment, allow peace to be your friend. Welcome it. Invite it in. As I repeat the word "peace" slowly in the next few minutes, allow it to reverberate deep into your consciousness, penetrating each and every fiber of your body, mind and soul. Feel it. Remember this vibration so you can pull it up and feel it at any time. Life is a journey to wholeness. Be a participant and contributor of raising the vibration of the earth.

Authenticity

Today is about being your authentic self. Your true self. Oftentimes we are concerned about what people think of us. We measure our success by what we do and what we have accumulated. Although those things make living easier on an egoic level, what really matters on a spiritual level is who we are. It seems that we get stuck in the material world and keep running on a hamster wheel where as one of the most important things is for us to stop for a few moments. Be in the present and put awareness on what is really important - being in harmony on a soul level.

Everyone has the teaching right in front of them, but most times people go about their daily lives, putting their consciousness on everything but that which serves them most. Do you not have five or ten minutes in the morning and evening to bring balance into your life? How many minutes or hours a day are spent watching TV, reading and tending to others in our household? Brushing and flossing our teeth, taking showers, getting dressed, cooking, eating and washing dishes are part of our daily routine, yet tending to our spirit is left for when there is time, elusive time.

This is not to chide you dear ones, but to gently prod you into feeding your soul. There are few other things that can gracefully bring your heart to purr like a symphony, clarify thoughts, bring balance to body, mind and spirit, allow you to feel your authentic self whereby your heart is open to loving your fellow men and women. If you really listen, you may eventually hear the divine power within you. The more you practice, the more you will feel the ever-loving companionship and connection to all that is.

I press upon you to think about these thoughts and carry on a spiritual practice that will serve you and your fellow beings. Every moment that you put yourself in balance, spirit lends itself to sending out loving vibrations to those around you. Our love for you is great and will be the same for you whether or not you follow these thoughts.

Presence

Many of us pay more attention to intense experiences rather than everyday ordinary moments. Love, excitement, pain, and sorrow. Positive or negative, both let us know we are alive. I will speak aloud while you follow along in silence.

I radiate and receive love.

I have vibrant health and unlimited energy.

I radiate and receive gratitude.

Everything is for my best and highest good.

Abundance flows effortlessly into my life.

I have unlimited resources in every area of my life.

I choose to forgive all in my life.

Peace

What is peace? It is the ability to accept all that is. To let go of what you think it should be. To steer one's ship loosely to allow for shifting to get to a place inside, that is open, allowing energy to flow freely. To be able to forgive, let go, accept, and be in the moment. To speak with honor by being truthful with everyone. Letting go of hearsay and rumors. To allow for differences among friends, family, peoples, countries. Peace comes with surrender.

PART VII

Epilogue

Epilogue

After reading The Gift, you may wonder, "Where do I go from here?" My reply is meditate because it assists in preparing us for everyday living. Starting with just ten minutes a day begins to rest the body and clear the mind. Research shows it can improve chronic pain, anxiety, stress and heart health. Try yoga, which also calms the mind while moving the body. Take a metaphysics class, experience a Reiki or hypnosis session. Each of these will further your knowledge of the unknown and perhaps ignite the thirst to seek more. Read books on the topics discussed.

Know that we are all students and teachers, seeing our reflection in those around us. I learned when someone irritates me, oftentimes, it's because there is something in them I can identify with - something I don't like in myself. Knowing this gives me the opportunity to look inward and ask, what am I supposed to learn from this?

I still have sensitivities due to chemical exposure years ago, catch colds and get the flu, but I continually strive to have more peace among the chaos. Being tranquil, meditating for hours without distraction is easy. The true test is experiencing peace while dealing with crises in our lives. I do not claim to have mastered this, although my periods of joy and appreciation are more frequent. Practicing patience, humility, and compassion raises the vibration of those around me, which in turn raises the vibration of the earth, as well as advances my own soul.

Working with people gives me unparalleled joy when they experience energy radiating through their bodies, are transported back to a previous life, or feel a level of relaxation far beyond what they thought was possible. I am elated when their universe widens to include a greater understanding that life is multi-dimensional and we are all connected.

I've pondered how it is possible to help others heal. The secret is simple; I believe it is a dual process between the giver and the receiver. I interpret it as an exchange of energy to get results. An unwritten contract of sincerity, openness, and intent that irresistibly draws love out of me and creates a space conducive to healing. This "agreement" in sacred space allows me to draw upon energies far beyond what I am solely capable of, which assist me in aiding the recipient.

My wish is that everyone realizes the powerful force within themselves. We are truly magnificent and amazing beings.

GLOSSARY

Channeling is a form of communication between humans and non-physical entities, angels, spirits or animals.

Mutual UFO Network, Inc., (MUFON) Newport Beach California was Founded in 1969. It is one of the most respected scientific organizations devoted to studying and researching UFO phenomena. MUFON sponsors and conducts worldwide conferences and symposia throughout the world.

National Investigations Committee on Unidentified Flying Objects (NICUFO) provides research and education on UFOs, Space and Science Phenomena. The Mutual UFO Network in California is also a scientific organization devoted to researching UFO phenomena as well as conducting conferences.

Reiki is the Japanese art of hands-on-healing based on the spiritual teachings of Mikao Usui early in the twentieth century. Reiki is derived from two Japanese words, rei (universal) and ki (life energy).

SUGGESTED READING

A Course in Miracles by Dr. Helen Schucman

Edgar Cayce The Sleeping Prophet by Jess Stearn

Hands of Light by Barbara Brennan

Heal Thyself – The Way to Healing Through Spirit by White
Eagle

Hope from the Other Side by George Anderson and Andrew
Barone

Lessons from the Light: Extraordinary Messages of Comfort
and

Love and Roses for David by Rob Grant

Saved by the Light by Dannion Brinkley

Strangers from the Pentagon: The UFO Conspiracy by Dr.
Frank E. Stranges

The Stranger at the Pentagon by Dr. Frank E. Stranges

The True History of Merlin the Magician by Anne Lawrence-
Mathers

There is a River by Thomas Segrue

Tibetan Book of the Dead by Graham Coleman and Thupten
Jinpa

Many Lives, Many Masters by Dr. Brian Weiss

56254463R10125

Made in the USA
Middletown, DE
21 July 2019